BATTERSEA

HERE FOR EVERY DOG AND CAT

A CAT A DAY

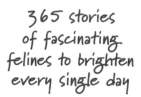

365 stories
of fascinating
felines to brighten
every single day

BATTERSEA
HERE FOR EVERY DOG AND CAT

A CAT A DAY

365 stories of fascinating felines to brighten every single day

CONTENTS

Battersea will always be here for every dog and cat, and has been since 1860.

Battersea takes dogs and cats in, gives them the expert care they need and finds them new homes that are just right for them.

They help pet owners make informed choices, provide training advice and campaign for changes in the law. They also help other rescue centres and charities at home and abroad because they want to be here for every dog and cat, wherever they are, for as long as they need Battersea.

Your purchase will help Battersea continue its important work. Thank you.

JANUARY

Cairo

Rapper Macklemore has a cat called Cairo who, he says, gives him the inspiration to help him write new material. When Macklemore introduced Cairo to his fans, he did so with the words 'Best decision I've made in a long time . . .' Macklemore (real name Benjamin Hammond Haggerty) released the album *The Language of My World* with its lead single 'Love Song' on January 1, 2005.

Percy

Celia Birtwell, the textile designer whose prints adorned the clothes of icons of the Swinging Sixties like Twiggy and Marianne Faithfull was born on this day in 1941. She married her long-time boyfriend and collaborator fashion designer Ossie Clark at Kensington Register Office in 1969. A year later David Hockney, the couple's best man, began work on his painting of the couple *Mr and Mrs Clark and Percy* which now hangs in the Tate Britain. Percy, the cat, sitting on Clark's lap, perhaps gives a clue to his character – a free spirit. In fact, Celia later said, the cat depicted is Blanche, Percy's mother. 'When she told me that, I told her, well, shut up, because Mr and Mrs Clark and Blanche doesn't sound as good as Mr and Mrs Clark and Percy,' Hockney said.

3 JANUARY

Formulino

The Imola racetrack is in the Emilia-Romagna region of Italy, about 25 miles east of Bologna. It also happens to be home to a very special cat called Formulino who is said to bring luck to the F1 drivers who race there. Formulino likes to hang in the pits and has even been featured in a F1 calendar shot. Apparently, drivers believe he brings them luck and so they will give the grey tabby a stroke before they get into their cars – with multiple world champion driver Lewis Hamilton even welcoming him into his Mercedes team garage one year. Timing, measured to the split second, is everything in F1 and on this day in 1957, the Hamilton watch company introduced the first-ever electric watch.

4 JANUARY

Pandy Paws

There are cats, cats and even more cats in the DreamWorks animated TV series *Gabby's Dollhouse*, which premiered on this day in 2021. She might be a little bit younger than the stereotypical 'cat lady', but Gabby is firmly Team Cat and with her sidekick, Pandy Paws, she has lots of cat-related adventures. Gabby uses a pair of magical cat ears to shrink down to a size small enough to go into her cat-themed dollhouse. The series, which ran for seven seasons, stars veteran voice actor Tara Strong as Kitty Fairy.

5 JANUARY

Tama

On this date in 2007, Tama the cat became the official stationmaster of Kishi station in Japan. Sweet-natured, pretty and a lover of cuddles, Tama had worked her way into commuters' affections and, at a ceremony, was presented with a gold tag for her collar stating her name and position. Her salary – all the cat food she could eat – was topped off with an office at the station with a cosy bed and litter tray and Sundays off. But Tama was more than just a pretty face. The 14-stop Kishigawa line had been under threat due to low passenger numbers, but was saved as Tama's fame grew thanks to media coverage and tourists came to Kishi. When Tama died aged 16 in 2015, thousands attended her funeral, but her paws were ably filled by her apprentice the equally beguiling Nitama.

6 JANUARY

Avery

It's a mystery even Sherlock Holmes, whose birthday fans celebrate on 6 January, might struggle to crack, with a very sneaky cat burglar at its heart. Over the summer of 2020, a grey and white cat from Bristol, called Avery, brought his owner Sally Bell a haul of eleven pairs of children's swimming goggles (including two pairs which were brand new with the price stickers still attached). 'I feel bad in case it's children who are being brought new goggles and they're getting into trouble because they keep going missing,' Sally said, knocking neighbours' doors and appealing for information on Facebook. No owners came forward, so Sally donated the goggles to a charity shop. Still, Avery's antics caused plenty of amusement online.

7 JANUARY

Tigra & Merlin

Star of *The Wicker Man* (the 2006 remake) psychological horror and comic-book lover, actor Nicolas Cage, has a Maine Coons cat called Tigra and another called Merlin, whom he rehomed in 2017 and now describes as his best friend. The lifelong cat lover who is the nephew of film director Francis Ford Coppola, says Merlin, who is a black Maine Coon, is not only his best friend but also 'like a son' to him. Nick often refers to just chilling at home, reading a book and hanging out with Merlin and adds, 'He's an unusual cat, he's very affectionate, he loves contact. And it's just kind of an amazing, loving, affectionate energy that's coming off that cat. He's a real sweetheart.'

8 JANUARY

Kitty Galore

In the family film *Cats and Dogs: the Revenge of Kitty Galore*, the two tribes put their usual differences aside and join forces to fight the threat of a spy cat gone rogue and now threatening world domination. The film has a soundtrack featuring the pop classic 'Get the Party Started', which was recorded by Shirley Bassey, who was born on this day in 1937. Cast members in the 2010 film, which grossed US$ 112.5 million at the box office, features actor and singer Bette Midler starring as Kitty Galore and Christina Applegate as Agent 47 at M.E.O.W.S.

9 JANUARY

Zarathustra

The trial of Joan of Arc commenced on this day in the French town of Rouens in 1431. There's a very famous illustration that shows the French warrior riding into battle, fully armoured and sat astride a white horse. But where does the cat fit into this story, you might ask? Well, he doesn't – at least not until artist Svetlana Petrova got involved some 600 years later. Svetlana creates artworks by taking digital images of famous paintings by the great artists and inserting her big ginger cat, called Zarathustra, into them. So in Svetlana's hands, Joan of Arc's noble white horse comically becomes a large ginger cat. Zarathustra also makes an appearance in Svetlana's unique takes on works by da Vinci, Dalí and Degas. As you can imagine, her artworks have become very popular among cat lovers online.

10 JANUARY

Masha

One cold night in the town of Obninsk near Moscow, a stray tabby cat called Masha found an abandoned baby left in a box on the doorstep on an apartment building. It was several degrees below freezing and, although the baby was bundled up, the cat climbed into the box to keep the child warm and sound the alarm. Resident Irene Lavrova was taking the rubbish out when she heard the loud meowing and went to investigate. Masha was known to the locals and her unusual behaviour alerted Irene, who took the baby to hospital. Doctors there said that without the extra warmth given by the cat, the child might not have survived the cold night.

Venus, Mercury & Mars

Did you know guitar legend Jimi Hendrix was a cat man? And not only that, he was a cat man with a penchant for naming his cats after the planets – hence, Venus, Mercury and Mars. It seems Jimi's love of felines started in childhood when his family had a pet cat called Withey. On this day in 1967, the Jimi Hendrix Experience recorded 'Purple Haze' at the De Lane Lea studio in London. This was the band's second single and featured some of Jimi's finest and most innovative playing, and the psychedelic track became one of the signature Hendrix hits.

Puss in Boots

The clever cat in this classic story hates seeing his penniless young master so miserable and downhearted, and decides to take matters into his own hands. The young man has inherited nothing but the talking cat following the death of his father, so Puss – who has the gift of being able to talk thanks to a pair of Magic Boots – lies that he is fantastically wealthy and must then find a way to cover up this deceit. Still a popular tale, *Puss in Boots* was already old when retold by the French author Charles Perrault, who was born on this day in 1628.

13 JANUARY

Mittens

In the comedy series *Schitt's Creek*, we meet a perfectly healthy cat called Mittens who, thanks to hypochondriac owner Doris, makes regular, almost weekly appearances at the local vet's clinic. The Emmy-nominated show, which won Best Comedy Series at the Canadian Screen Awards in 2016, was penned by Eugene and Daniel Levy, the father and son duo who also star. The first episode aired on this day in 2015 and the series – which tells the story of a wealthy couple and their two grown-up children who lose everything and have to cope with life in a small town – became an international hit.

14 JANUARY

Antonia

In a photograph by society snapper Cecil Beaton, born on this day in 1904, Christabel Lady Aberconway and her cat Antonia are pictured, eyes focused on the distance. 'This is not the soul's awakening but myself and my personal cat listening to a maddening bird,' she wrote. In 1949 Lady Aberconway wrote *A Dictionary of Cat Lovers*, a compendium of anecdotes about famous fans of felines and their pets.

15 JANUARY

Museum Mike

Mike the cat spent nearly 20 years guarding the gates of the British Museum in London, gaining fame in that time and even being featured in *Time* magazine. He now has his own entry on Wikipedia, which states that Mike was trained for this important role by a predecessor, who is said to have walked up to the then Keeper of Egyptian antiquities in 1908 and dropped the gift of Mike (a kitten) at his feet. The story is that the predecessor trained Mike to stalk and catch pigeons, which the cats would deliver to the housekeeper, who would reward the cats with food and then release the dazed birds back to the streets of London. The British Museum opened this day in 1759.

16 JANUARY

Fusker, The Fluff & the Bounce

The British TV presenter James May is a cat lover and currently lives in London with his partner and two rescue cats called The Fluff and The Bounce. The former *Top Gear* presenter regularly shares images of the cats on his social media and will frequently down tools and say he's had to stop work for the day because one of the cats has decided to visit and sit on his computer keyboard – something many cat lovers will recognise. James once astounded his fellow *Top Gear* presenters when he told them he loved his previous cat, Fusker, above all else – including his vintage Bentley car!

17 JANUARY

Catwoman

American singer Eartha Kitt, born on this day in 1927, played Catwoman in the 1960s' TV series of *Batman* – and she was a cat woman in real life too. Her cat Jinx was a constant companion, even joining her in radio studios for interviews and hanging out in her dressing room while she was on stage at the theatre. 'I think people can learn a lot from cats,' Eartha, who was also a powerful advocate for rescue cats, said. 'They're clean, neat, quiet, graceful and independent.'

18 JANUARY

Tigger

Tigger, like all the animals in the *Winnie-the-Pooh* stories, was based on a stuffed toy tiger that belonged to writer A.A. Milne's young son, Christopher Robin. *Winnie-the-Pooh* actually first appeared as a children's story commissioned by the *London Evening News* for publication on Christmas Eve in 1925 and big cat Tigger, who is full of energy and verve, made his screen debut in the 1968 short Disney film *Winnie the Pooh and the Blustery Day*. A.A. Milne was born on this day in 1882.

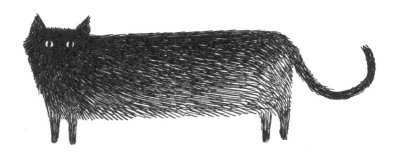

19 JANUARY

Smelly Cat

Who can forget the iconic song 'Smelly Cat', which we first heard in episode six of the second season of the hit show *Friends*? But what you may not know is that along with Lisa Kudrow, who played Phoebe Buffay and performs the song in the show, one of the iconic tune's co-writers was a serious rocker and a member of the British-American band of the late 1970s and '80s, the Pretenders. That rocker is none other than Chrissie Hynde, who is herself a cat lover. The Pretenders had their first UK No. 1 hit with the song 'Brass in Pocket', which topped the charts on this day in 1980.

20 JANUARY

Hollywood Hager

Hollywood is a very glamorous name for a rescue kitten, but this little cat is both political and entertainment royalty as the family pet of Jenna Bush Hager, one of the daughters of former US President George W. Bush, who was sworn in as the 43rd president on this day in 2001. Jenna is a journalist and author and the co-host of the NBC news show *Today with Hoda & Jenna.* Introducing her new kitten on Instagram, Jenna wrote, 'My eyes are red from cat allergies, but I love her!'

21 JANUARY

Crystal & Misty Blue

Crystal the cat belongs to Hollywood actor John Travolta, who rehomed her in March 2021. Animal lover John shot to stardom in the 1977 film *Saturday Night Fever*, the soundtrack of which started a 24-week run at the top of the US album chart on this day in 1978. The record went on to win Album of the Year at the Grammy Awards the following year and eventually sold more than 40 million copies worldwide, making it one of the bestselling soundtracks albums of all time, second only to *The Bodyguard* (1992). The star of that film, the late Whitney Houston, was a cat lover too and had a cat called Misty Blue.

Lucas the Kop Cat

Named by fans, Lucas the Kop Cat is a snow leopard (well, someone dressed up in a snow leopard costume) and the mascot for Leeds United, the English football team. The choice of a white big cat is said to have been made in homage to the team's white and blue uniform, which was first chosen in 1919. Lucas the Kop Cat became the club's mascot in 2005. And on this day in 1927, sports broadcaster and rugby union player Teddy Wakelam gave the first live radio commentary of a football match, when Arsenal played Sheffield United at Highbury.

Wendell

Elvis Presley had a huge heart when it came to animals and it's said that no creature that found its way to Graceland would be turned away; instead, Elvis and his entourage would find a new home for the animal. Wendell was a cat the rock star took in and named after Wendell Corey, his co-star in the 1957 film *Loving You*. On this day in 1986, Elvis was one of the first stars inducted into the Rock & Roll Hall of Fame, alongside Little Richard, Chuck Berry, James Brown, Ray Charles, Sam Cooke, Fats Domino, the Everly Brothers, Buddy Holly and Jerry Lee Lewis.

24 JANUARY

Eve & Royal Wallace

Singer Ellie Goulding has two cats. Aqua-eyed Royal Wallace, who she has owned since 2015, is a leopard-print Bengal and Eve, who she adopted in 2017. Don't be fooled by the name because Eve, who is white with a grey-black tint on his paws and ears, is actually a male. (Word is Eve got his name because he joined Ellie's family on New Year's Eve.) Ellie admits she was a cat lady even before she got her own cat. Back in 2013, the TV Talk show host Ellen DeGeneres (another cat lover) noted that the 'Love Me Like You Do' singer posted a lot of random cat pictures she found on the Internet. 'I'm obsessed now. I never thought I was gonna be one of those people who was gonna post photos of a lot of animals, and now I am. I'm Catwoman,' the singer joked. 'Love Me Like You Do' debuted on the Billboard Hot 100 chart on this day in 2015.

25 JANUARY

Sappho

'Kind old ladies assure us that cats are often the best judges of character,' Virginia Woolf, born on this day in 1882, wrote. 'A cat will always go to a good man, they say.' Virginia, perhaps with feline-like astute judgement, adored cats. With her first pay cheque as a journalist, she admitted that 'instead of spending that sum upon bread and butter, rent, shoes and stockings, or butcher's bills, I went out and bought a cat.' Sappho features in five photographs held by Harvard Library, napping in the sunshine and being petted.

26 JANUARY

Old Hollywood Cats

When art collector Klaus Moeller acquired the rights to millions of photographic negatives of Old Hollywood film stars which had been stashed for decades in a filing cabinet, he stumbled on a treasure trove of images showing just how much these stars loved their cats. There were images of screen legend Elizabeth Taylor with her cat and others showing Jane Fonda in bed with her kittens, and the Italian star Claudia Cardinale feeding her cats. Elizabeth Taylor's route to Hollywood stardom was kicked off in earnest with the release of the film *National Velvet*, on this day in 1944. Starring Mickey Rooney, the film tells the story of a horse-obsessed young woman and her dreams of racing her new horse, whom she names The Pie.

27 JANUARY

The Cheshire Cat

With his distinctive wide-mouthed grin, the Cheshire Cat is, of course, a character in Lewis Carrols book *Alice's Adventures in Wonderland* and widely considered to have been a kind of guiding spirit to the young Alice, since he is the character who leads her to both the March Hare's House and the Mad Hatter's tea party. Carrol was born this day in 1832 and says he first saw the face of a smiling cat carved into the wall of the tower at Brimstage Hall, a fourteenth-century building in the Wirral (formerly Cheshire). The cat's superpower is the ability to appear and just as suddenly disappear!

28 JANUARY

Queso, Carl, Charlie & Mr Peeps

Proud cat owner Kesha has four rescue cats, Queso, Carl, Charlie and Mr Peeps. Carl is a Persian who first made his debut on the performer's social media early in 2019, Queso and Charlie are both Maine Coons and Mr Peeps was a stray kitten that Kesha is said to have found in Russia. She brought him back to the United States where he went on to appear in her 'Crazy Kids' music video. The American singer/songwriter, rapper and actor received two Grammy nominations at the 60th Grammy Awards, which were held in Madison Square Garden on this day in 2018.

29 JANUARY

'Caturday'

Tony Gonsolin, baseball pitcher for the Los Angeles Dodgers, has always been a big 'cat man', and the team's Saturday practice sessions, during which the pitcher embraces his 'inner cat', are now known as 'Caturdays'. Once described in a World Series promo as 'part man, part cat', the Major League player explains that the cat tropes all started when his pitching coach, knowing how much the player loved cats, left him a $5 shirt with a cat on it in his locker room one Friday. Gonsolin wore the shirt to stretch the following day, which then became known as Caturday. And the rest, as they say, is history . . . as is the fact that on this day in 1936, the very first inductees into the Baseball Hall of Fame were announced.

Mochi

Mochi is a Japanese bobtail cat who stars in the Disney animated film *Big Hero 6*. He belongs to brothers Hiro and Tadashi and their Aunt Cass (voiced by Maya Rudolph), who is raising the boys. As it happens, Aunt Cass owns a café called the Lucky Cat Café. Most of Mochi's appearances in the film show her with her human companions, enjoying their company, so it's fair to say this is one happy fictional cat. The film was released in the UK on this day in 2015.

Cleo

Cleo, a rescue cat from Surrey, was the hero of her home on this day in 2013, enjoying a steady supply of cat treats as a reward for saving her owner's life. A few days earlier, Pauline Jenkins was watching *Coronation Street* when the normally laidback Cleo began yowling and howling. 'What do you want?' Pauline asked, confused. 'You've had dinner.' Tortoiseshell Cleo stared at Pauline intently – then dashed, still yowling, upstairs. Pauline followed her into the bedroom to find her husband Richard clutching his chest, having a heart attack. He was rushed to hospital for emergency surgery. 'If it wasn't for Cleo raising the alarm – well, I couldn't think of it,' Pauline said. As Richard recovered back home, Cleo didn't leave his side and, a year later, was honoured with an award.

FEBRUARY

1 FEBRUARY

Granpa Rex Allen

The brother of the world's oldest known cat, Crème Puff (*see* 27 August), Granpa Rex Allen also lived to a ripe old age: 34 years and 2 months. Granpa's owner, cat lover Jake Perry, said one of the reasons his cats lived so long was because they never had time to get bored. He turned the garage of his Austin, Texas home into a cinema which played nature documentaries for the cats, and also built play stairs into the walls of his home so the cats always had somewhere to jump and climb. Granpa, who was born on this day in 1964, was posthumously awarded a 'Cat of the Year' award in 1999.

Mr Winkers

Here's a clever way to make sure your cat has a starring role at your wedding – get a replica ice sculpture made. That's exactly what one couple did after learning their wedding venue package included an ice sculpture. The artwork faithfully replicated their rescue cat, named Mr Winkers because he only has one eye. Ice is the theme for this chilly February entry because on this day in 1814, the last of the River Thames Frost Fairs ended. The fairs became popular between the 17th and 19th centuries – also know as the Little Ice Age – when the river frequently froze.

Miss Moppet

The Story of Miss Moppet is a children's book written and illustrated by Beatrix Potter. It features a little kitten called Miss Moppet, who decides to tease a mouse which has been having a fine old time teasing her. In one scene, the kitten, who has bumped her head on a cupboard while chasing the mouse, decides to tie an old duster over her head like a bandage. She then sits stock-still in front of the fire until the little mouse can't resist creeping closer to see what's wrong. It's a clever play on well-known phrases, but this time it is the cat sitting 'as quiet as a mouse' and curiosity that gets the better of the mouse. The best known of all the Beatrix Potter animal characters is, of course, Peter Rabbit, and that character and his story was turned into a children's film that was released on this day in 2018.

Patsy

The American aviator Charles Lindbergh, born on this day in 1902, welcomed his cat Patsy into his life after the stray was found in an airport hangar. Occasionally Patsy went along for the ride in Lindbergh's planes, but she did not accompany him on his most famous flight – the world's first solo non-stop transatlantic crossing, from New York to Paris in 1927. A 1930 Spanish stamp, said to be the first ever featuring a cat, commemorated Lindbergh's feat with Patsy, grounded, gazing up at his plane as it took off.

Zen Cats

Anyone who has a cat and who practises yoga or meditation will tell you there's nothing cats like more than a spiritual vibe! Cat lover and Beatles star George Harrison was a big fan of meditation, so when he took his son, Dhani, for coaching at the Leander rowing club in Henley-on-Thames, he'd sit on a bench at the end of the Japanese Garden at Friar Park to meditate. And whenever he did that, the neighbourhood cats would find their way into the grounds through a gap in the fence next to Badgemore Primary school and sit quietly watching the Beatle as he zoned out. On this day in 1962, fellow cat lover Ringo Starr made his first appearance with the Beatles.

Meredith Grey, Olivia Benson & Benjamin Button

Megastar Taylor Swift is a huge cat lover and has at least three cats – that we know of. Meredith is named after Dr. Meredith Grey from *Grey's Anatomy* and Olivia is named for the character in *Law & Order: Special Victims Unit*. Benjamin – named after the film starring Brad Pitt – has a credit on online film database IMDb for his role in the music video for Taylor's single 'ME!'. The film from which his name is taken is *The Curious Case of Benjamin Button*, which tells the strange story of a man who ages in reverse, and was released in the UK on this day in 2009.

7 FEBRUARY

Montgomery (Monty) & D'Artagnan

Actor Robert Downey Jr. and his wife, Susan, have two cats, Montgomery and D'Artagnan, and Robert says he just can't imagine life without the duo. Best known for his role as Tony Stark in the *Iron Man* franchise, he also played Dr John Dolittle in the 2020 film *The Voyage of Doctor Dolittle*. And when asked what question he would ask his cats if he really could talk to the animals, the actor fired back, 'I would ask Monty, "Why do you wake up Mrs Downey at 5.30 a.m. every morning and how can we fix this?"' The actor added he would do some kind of deal with the kitten.

8 FEBRUARY

Jasmine, Dexter, Loki, Angie, Fluffy, Fluffy Jr, Fluffy Sr, Bad Leroy, Jeff & Princess Unikitty

There's more than a touch of a feline thread running through the family favourite *The Lego Movie* in which all the characters – and the many cats – are made almost entirely from Lego bricks. We meet our first LEGO felines when our hero, Emmet Brickowski, bumps into Mrs Sherry Scratchen-Post aka 'The Cat Lady' on his way to work at a construction site. She has many, many cats, including the ten listed above. But the film also features a very unique cat-unicorn hybrid called Princess Unikitty who becomes one of Emmet's biggest allies and defenders. *The Lego Movie 2: The Second Part*, which saw the citizens of Bricksburg facing a new threat from DUPLO alien invaders, was released on this day in 2019.

9 FEBRUARY

Willow

There's a long history of pets at the White House and Willow is the latest in that long line after being adopted by the First Lady and wife of Joe Biden, Jill, who named the cat after her hometown, Willow Grove, Pennsylvania. Jill and Willow first met when she was giving a speech and the grey tabby jumped on stage. It was love at first sight . . . Biden is not the only President with a love of pets; other animal-loving examples include John Quincy Adams, who became the sixth President of the United States on this day in 1825, and John F. Kennedy, who owned a grey cat called Tom Kitten (see 29 May) alongside a rabbit, ponies, hamsters, dogs and more besides!

10 FEBRUARY

White Heather

Queen Victoria – who was the first Royal patron of Battersea – married the love of her life, Prince Albert of Saxe-Coburg and Gotha, on this day in 1840. When Albert unexpectedly died in 1861 at the age of just 42, leaving his wife bereft, she took solace in offering a home to many cats, but her favourite over the years was apparently a White Persian cat called White Heather. The Queen left instructions that the little cat should continue to live a life of luxury after her own death and that's exactly what happened, with White Heather living out her days in style at Buckingham Palace.

MC Skat Kat

MC Skat Kat is a rapping animated cat superstar who stars opposite pop singer Paula Abdul in her video for the 1989 song 'Opposites Attract', which shows the duo doing a move known as the Skat Strut. Paula, who went on to be one of the original judges for *American Idol*, serving from 2002 to 2009, had another hit in 1989 with the song 'Straight Up', which entered the US singles charts on this day and stayed at the top for three weeks. It was the second of her three No. 1 singles that year.

Fat Louie

The cat that stars as Mia's cat in the *Princess Diaries* film franchise belongs to the star Anne Hathaway, and is her pet cat in real life. The cat is called Fat Louie. In fact, the role of the cat in the films was played not just by Louie but by four different cats who all brought a different skill set to the role – among other skills there was one who would jump on demand, one who could sit perfectly still, and one who sits on the envelope at the end of the first film. Anne Hathaway also starred in the romantic comedy *Valentine's Day*, which was released on this day in 2010.

Marjaryasana

Marjaryasana, more commonly known as the cat pose, is one of the most popular poses in many different types of yoga class, along with another feline-inspired position, the cat stretch. The pose is designed to warm up the back, shoulders and hips and gives a great stretch to the lumbar, thoracic and cervical spine to help increase mobility and prepare the body for movement. Domestic cats in yoga-practising households tend to look on unimpressed at our attempts to mimic their movements!

14 FEBRUARY

Cats

Oscar-winning director Tom Hooper reimagined Andrew Lloyd-Webber's record-breaking feline musical to bring a more contemporary flavour to the story of T. S. Eliot's *Old Possum's Book of Practical Cats,* first published in 1939. Starring James Corden, Judi Dench, Idris Elba, Jennifer Hudson, Rebel Wilson and pop star Taylor Swift, the film also showcases a world-class cast of dancers from classical ballet to hip-hop, street dance to jazz.

15 FEBRUARY

Sir John Langborn

The English philosopher Jeremy Bentham, born on this day in 1748, conferred various titles on his cat. As a youngster the feline, who attended all of Bentham's important meetings and had a taste for macaroni, was known as Sir John Langborn. 'In his early days he was a frisky, inconsiderate and, to say the truth, somewhat profligate gentleman,' wrote John Browning, editor of 11 volumes of Jeremy Bentham's work. 'But, tired at last, like Solomon, of pleasures and vanities, he became sedate and thoughtful – took to the church, laid down his knightly title and was installed as the Reverend John Langborn.'

16 FEBRUARY

Tomkins

Tomkins is the fictional cat who belonged to the real historical figure Oliver Cromwell in a book called *Cromwell's Cat*. The author, John Livesey, uses the cat as the literary device that allows Cromwell to reflect on the years from 1638 to 1658, which saw his rise through the military ranks, a civil war and his installation as Lord Protector of the country. The book sees Cromwell chew over all these events – and more – with his cat. This day in 1646 marked the Battle of Torrington in North Devon, which was the last major battle of the First English Civil War.

17 FEBRUARY

Dorito

Ed Sheeran and his wife Cherry are a cat-loving couple who like to name their rescue kittens after their favourite foods – in this case a tortilla crisp snack. Dorito, an orange and white tabby, has now amassed some 260K (and rising) Instagram followers in an account dedicated to Ed's two cats and followed by their superstar owner's faithful fans. Today is Ed's birthday.

18 FEBRUARY

Apollinaris, Beelzebub, Blatherskite, Buffalo Bill and friends

It has been said that the American writer Mark Twain, whose classic novel *Adventures of Huckleberry Finn* was published on this day in 1885, much preferred cats to people. He had many cats over his lifetime, only some of whom are named above and all of whom he adored. The author often gave cameo roles to cats in his books, including a cat called Peter in *Tom Sawyer*. And he once wrote, 'If man could be crossed with the cat, it would improve man, but it would deteriorate the cat.' There is a special word for a love of cats: *ailurophilia*!

19 FEBRUARY

Marie Antoinette

Marie Antoinette is a fictional cat who belongs to her elderly owner Mrs Patty Ponder whom we meet on the very first page of the New York Times bestselling book, *Big Little Lies*, inspiration for the hit drama of the same name. Patty is speaking aloud to the cat who is dozing on the couch and who, according to the author Liane Moriarty, is not particularly interested in what Patty is saying. Produced by and starring Hollywood big-hitters Reese Witherspoon and Nicole Kidman, the screen adaptation premiered on this day in 2017.

Speckled Cat

'The Cat' (who happens to be speckled) is a 1970 silkscreen image created by the American artist Gloria Vanderbilt, who was born on this day in 1924. Described as an artist, author, actor, fashion designer, heiress and socialite, New Yorker Gloria carried the name of the Vanderbilt family, who made their money in shipping and on the railroads and who came to prominence in what has been called the Gilded Age.

Kedi

Istanbul is home to countless stray cats, fed by the cat-loving population, and they were celebrated in the documentary film *Kedi*, which premiered in the city on this day in 2016. *Kedi* (which means 'cat' in Turkish) follows seven street cats, each with distinct personalities, like Duman the Gentleman and Gamsiz the Player. 'We found cats in hammams, museums, mosques,' says film-maker Ceyda Torun. 'Cats provide this wonderful opportunity for people in Istanbul to pick a moment to be affectionate with a being that doesn't judge them.' The feline-focused film was a surprise hit at the box office, charming cinema audiences the world over.

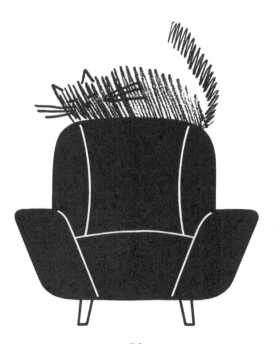

22 FEBRUARY

Oscar

Oscar is the subject of the book *Making Rounds with Oscar*, written by health researcher and geriatrician Dr David Dosa, who worked with patients at the Steere House Nursing and Rehabilitation Center in Providence, Rhode Island. Not long after arriving at the hospice, Oscar started to show an extraordinary talent for knowing which patients needed comforting the most. Dr Dosa and the staff noticed that Oscar would move in with a patient just as they neared the end of their life, somehow seeming to know when their time was almost up. According to the book, he did this some 30 times in a row. Nobody knows how Oscar knew who needed him the most, but we do know that this little cat would honour those approaching the end of their lives by offering whatever comfort he could by their side.

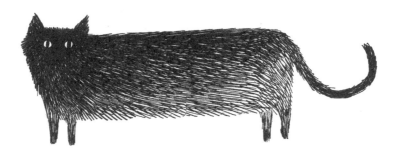

Robot Therapy Cats

Many cats have a calming effect on their owners – and even others who they will accept some stroking and fuss from. So it's perhaps no surprise that an American company manufactures robot cats to use as a form of therapy. The built-in sensors mean the robot cats will purr and meow when stroked. In 2021, the Wakefield Rotary club in the North of England began fundraising to buy robot cats for members of the community who were isolated and alone. On this day in 1905, a Chicago attorney named Paul Harris and three other businessmen met for lunch to form the Rotary Club; it was the world's first service club.

Towser

On this day in 1965, tortoiseshell Towser was hard at work, as she was every other day of the year, keeping the Glenturret Distillery in Perthshire mouse-free. Towser was often pictured roaming among the whisky casks in the local press and her pawprints were added as an illustration to some of the distillery's bottles while local legend talks of her mouse-catching prowess. When Towser died in 1987, at the ripe old age of 24, a bronze statue was erected in her honour at the distillery and she was replaced by Amber, a total flop in terms of catching mice, often running away when one appeared, but a great favourite in the visitor centre. Now Turret and Glen have taken on the distillery cats' mantle although, with barley no longer malted on site, their role involves less mousing and more schmoozing.

25 FEBRUARY

Spartacus

At the Tesco store in Dunfermline, Scotland, there was no doubting the identity of Spartacus – he was the black and white cat who visited every day for five years, delighting staff and customers alike. Spartacus, usually to be found gazing down on the store from the tallest tower of merchandise or getting comfy among the pillows, was such a star he was even given his own bed and a mention, as in-store cat, on the list of in-store amenities posted at the entrance. When Spartacus and his family moved away in March 2023, staff and shoppers held a fundraiser for a local cat rescue in his name. Services Manager at Tesco Duloch Park, Lynne Louden, told a local paper: 'Everybody is so gutted that he's leaving. They just absolutely love seeing him when they come in, the bairns come in, elderly folk come in, just to see him, and it's just not going to be the same without him.'

Bagpuss

On this day in 1974, the third episode of *Bagpuss* aired – only 13 were ever made but the tales of a 'baggy and a bit loose at the seams' pink-and-white striped cat were voted the most popular children's series ever in 1999. Affable, sleepy Bagpuss lived in the window of the shop where Emily fixed lost things she'd found (jewels in this third episode), along with his friends – the singing mice and know-it-all Professor Yaffle, the woodpecker-shaped wooden bookend. Bagpuss' bright pink stripes were a happy accident – he was supposed to be marmalade in colour but something went wrong at a fabric dyeing shop in Folkestone. He now lives in Canterbury Heritage Museum with the Clangers, stars of another 1970s children's television show.

Cassius

'Please come back!' film star Elizabeth Taylor, born on this day in 1932, implored her missing cat Cassius in a 1974 letter. Taylor was a celebrated animal lover and was distraught when Cassius disappeared, leaving no stone unturned in her search for him. She even wrote him a letter, detailing how much she missed him. 'I remember the sweet smell of your fur against my neck when I was deeply in trouble,' she wrote, 'and how, somehow you made it better – you knew!'

28 FEBRUARY

Tink

A Shropshire family were thanking their lucky stars on this day in 2016 after their rescue cat saved them from a house fire. Tink the tortoiseshell, who normally slept like a log on the sofa, jumped on to owner Claire Hopkinson's legs at dawn, waking her up. Claire opened her eyes to find the bedroom filled with smoke. Ringing 999, she woke her family and they raced outside, but as six fire engines arrived there was no sign of Tink. Then a fireman emerged from the flames, carrying her, lifeless, in his arms. He held a tiny cat-sized oxygen mask over her face and she coughed. Any longer in the house, said the fireman, and the smoke would have killed her. Tink was honoured for her bravery a few months later. 'If it wasn't for Tink the outcome could have been horrific,' Claire said. 'She really is our hero.'

29 FEBRUARY

Morris

This week in 1935 Clark Gable was celebrating winning what was to be his only Oscar as Best Actor in *It Happened One Night*. He didn't need to act when it came to cats, though – he loved them and was often photographed with his Siamese. Decades later, a cat called Morris was praised for sharing Gable's acting abilities. Apparently in the late 1960s an animal trainer spotted Morris' potential in the cat rescue shelter and took him for a casting call for a cat food brand. According to the trainer, he 'jumped on the table and walked right up to the art director, the big cheese, and bumped him in the head. Then Morris just sat back. The art director said: "This is the Clark Gable of cats."' Morris went on to star in nearly 60 adverts and two movies over a ten-year career.

MARCH

Sushi & Tuna

Justin Bieber, who celebrates his birthday today, is a fan of giving his cats foodie names, having owned pets called Sushi and Tuna. And it would seem Justin himself is a popular name among cat owners: lots of kitties are named after the singer. One of them, known on social media by his full name Justin Bieber the Cat, is a 'talking tabby' who can apparently recognise 40-plus words and who uses a special push-button speech mat to clearly communicate with his owner.

Solomon

You may not have imagined James Bond would have a soft spot for cats but in real life, superstar actor Daniel Craig, who played the MI6 secret agent for five films, from *Casino Royale* in 2006 to *No Time to Die* in 2021, has a cat called Solomon who is no stranger to being among acting or fashion royalty. Solomon was sitting happily on Daniel's knee when he did a video interview with M (Dame Judi Dench) for *Vogue* magazine. And in a case of life imitating art, Solomon may be named after the white cat that we often see sitting in the lap of Bond villain Blofeld lap, and whose name we finally learn in *For Your Eyes Only* (1981). Today is Daniel Craig's birthday.

3 MARCH

Merlin

There's a world record for the tallest cat, the longest cat and the longest-lived cat, but did you know there's also one for the world's loudest purr? That happens to belong to a rescue cat from Devon called Merlin, who holds the current Guinness World Record for being the loudest domestic cat after registering a sound of 67.8 decibels, equivalent to the sound of a shower running and louder than a washing machine! The decibel system is named after Alexander Graham Bell, who also invented the modern telephone and was born this day 1847.

4 MARCH

Slippers

On this day in 1905, Theodore Roosevelt was inaugurated for a second term as President of the United States – good news for his menagerie of animals who enjoyed life in the White House. A confident soul, Slippers was a blue-grey tabby with six fingers on his right paw, who invited himself to state dinners. In January 1906, Roosevelt offered his arm to the British ambassador's wife to escort her from dinner to the after-dinner concert when he spied Slippers snoozing in the middle of the hall ahead. Rather than move the cat napper, he manoeuvred his companion in a wide circle around Slippers, all the other officials and dinner guests making the same loop around Slippers in his wake. Slippers repaid the favour, keeping the President company while he read in the evenings.

5 MARCH

Smudge

Barbra Streisand's 'Evergreen', from the film *A Star is Born*, became No. 1 in America on this day in 1976. The song holds another, rather more quirky, accolade – it reunited Smudge the cat from East Sussex with her owners. Ann Tillot loved the song, often practising it around the house for her performances at karaoke. And she had one big fan. 'When I sang "Evergreen",' Smudge sprinted from wherever she was in the house to leap on my lap, rub her face against mine and lick me,' Ann said. So, when Smudge went missing in February 2016, Ann pounded the streets singing 'Evergreen', hoping the song would bring Smudge running. Sure enough, after three weeks: 'The fronds of a bush moved and Smudge's little face peeked out,' Ann explained. 'I might not pack Broadway with fans but I drew the only crowd that mattered – Smudge.'

6 MARCH

Zoe & Davenport

Zoe and Davenport are two cats who sit in a tree outside the Mutt & Stuff school for dogs, where they share a running commentary about what the dogs are doing. The duo exchange jokes and often laugh so hard they fall out of the tree. Happily, they never come to harm but find that even funnier! Zoe, who is blue, is performed by Donna Kimball. Davenport, who is purple, is played by Drew Massey. *Mutt & Stuff* is an American children's TV series which ran on the Nick Jr. channel, first airing on this day in 2015.

Jean Burden

'A dog is prose; a cat is a poem' – and that's why American poet Jean Burden found her muse among the many cats of her company. Apparently, as a child, she rehomed a stray kitten who befriended her while she was sitting on the porch reading, and it's from there that her love of cats sparked. Certainly she understood their nature. 'Prowling his own quiet backyard or asleep by the fire, he is still only a whisker away from the wilds,' she wrote. Burden's *A Celebration of Cats: An Anthology of Poems* was published in 1974. She wasn't just interested in celebrating cats in poetry, though – she was pets editor of *Woman's Day* magazine and wrote about their practical care through books such as *The Woman's Day Book of Hints for Cat Owners*. In 2023 on 7 March, the Center for Contemporary Poetry and Poetics at California State University, LA, remembered Jean with a poetry reading in her honour.

Trim

If you ever visit the Mitchell Library in Sydney, you will see a statue of a man called Matthew Flinders, an English cartographer and seafarer who helped to map Australia. Matthew was a cat lover and, if you take the time to look up to the window ledge behind him, you will spot the bronze figure of his faithful cat Trim, who travelled the seas with his master. Trim was born in 1799 on HMS *Reliance* and so lived a life full of adventure. He once fell overboard but instead of panicking, learned to swim — and when the crew threw him a rescue rope he calmly climbed to safety, earning the respect of all aboard the ship. Trim was the first cat to circumnavigate Australia and his statue was erected in 1996. The Mitchell Library first opened on this day in 1910.

Micka

As the 'First Cat' of the Czech Republic, we can assume that Micka holds more than a little political sway. She featured in the 2023 election campaign of Czech President Petr Paval, who took office on this day in 2023 and is often photographed in his owner's arms. The new president reported that voters loved seeing her by his side during his campaigning and he believes her presence, along with his habitual flannel shirt, helped him win office. The little rescue was originally found by the family's dog, Bob, stranded in a snowdrift in 2012. Now she lives in Prague Castle.

10 MARCH

The little red cat

In the early 1970s, Ali MacGraw was cinema's golden girl, starring with Ryan O'Neal in the weepie romance *Love Story*, released this week in the UK in 1970. But, since leaving Hollywood in the mid-1980s, MacGraw has devoted her time to animal activism, her pets and yoga. In her book *Moving Pictures*, written about her life at the age of 50, MacGraw talks of the contentment she has found in the simple routines of her farmhouse in Maine. And, she writes with relief: 'I have coaxed the little red cat to eat, in spite of the fact she isn't feeling well.' The cat also inspires her writing: 'I find it easiest to recapture moments like these when the sunlight falls in a certain way, or in little things like the marmalade cat that is tumbling about in my garden.'

Tibs

On this day in 2010, the Royal Mail issued a set of stamps, featuring seven dogs and three cats rehomed by Battersea, to celebrate the home's 150th anniversary. Cats have been friends to the Royal Mail for a long time, since they were first employed in post offices in the 1860s to protect parcels from rats and mice having a nibble in the hope they might contain food – which they often did. Cats were paid for this important work, their wages rising from a shilling a week in the 1860s to £2 a week by the 1980s. The most famous and diligent Post Office cats was Tibs, who worked at PO Headquarters for 14 years in the 1950s and '60s. 'Tibs the Great is No More' read the headline in *The Post Office Magazine* when he died in November 1964.

The Cat in the Hat

The Cat in the Hat is an iconic children's book written and illustrated by the American author, Theodor Geisel, using his now world-famous pen name Dr. Seuss. The book was published on this day in 1957. It's no exaggeration to say *The Cat in the Hat* is somewhat eccentric and when he decides to visit home-alone kids Sally and Sam, whose mum is out for the day, all manner of chaos ensues to brighten up what was a dull and rainy day. The book was such a success, it had sold over a million copies by 1960 and 40-something years later, in 2001, *Publishers Weekly* ranked the book as No. 9 on its list of bestselling children's books of all time!

13 MARCH

Teddy

Here's a cat who used up one of his nine lives when he found himself buried under rubble after a gas explosion at the family home in South Wales on this day in 2023. Ragdoll Teddy had been sitting on the sofa next to his human, Claire Griffiths-Bennett, who was rushed to hospital after the blast and feared the worst for her cat, left behind at the scene. Incredibly, rescue workers heard Teddy the following day and tried to coax him out, though it wasn't until his owner went home a full week later and whistled for him that he finally reappeared. Rescue workers described Teddy as 'dusty and a little cross' after his ordeal, but clearly very happy to be back in the arms of his owner.

14 MARCH

Tiger

Born on this day in 1879, German scientist Albert Einstein, known as the father of modern physics, shared his study with a number of feline companions over the years, including Tiger, who became depressed when it rained. 'I know what's wrong, dear fellow,' Einstein told his pet. 'But I don't know how to turn it off.' Tiger also became jealous, Einstein wrote, when he heard of a cat in New York who'd been named Albert Einstein in honour of his master. 'The reason is,' Einstein explained in a letter to his feline namesake's owner, 'that his own name "Tiger" does not express, as in your case, the close kinship to the Einstein family.'

15 MARCH

Gladstone

This time of year marks the final weeks of the UK's financial year, and the time that the government announces the Budget – with the 2023 Budget delivered on this day. You may think it is the Chancellor of the Exchequer who runs the nation's finances in Britain, but for a while the real power behind the throne was a black cat called Gladstone, who lived among the civil servants working for HM Treasury. So fond were the workers of Gladstone – a rescue from Battersea – that many of them drank their morning tea from mugs emblazoned with his whiskery face. Gladstone would send Christmas cards featuring a photo of himself to family and friends, and before he retired on health grounds, Gladstone was known as the best mouser of all the Westminster cats.

16 MARCH

Monique

On this day in 2020, a shy tabby cat called Monique moved to her new home after 130 days at Battersea. Monique created headlines around the world when staff at Battersea organised a birthday party for her, hoping that potential rehomers might pop by to say hello. Adnan from Lewisham spotted her and applied to rehome her. They were the perfect companions. Six months after rehoming Monique, Adnan said: 'She's very talkative and greets me every morning and can be very bossy when she wants treats. She follows me around the house, pawing at me for scratches and giving me headbutts for cuddles. She was initially keen to jump in my lap (which was interesting when I was working) but has now decided that her many napping spots are much more comfortable and will instead summon me for scratches.'

Victoria & Jennyanydots

Cats is the 2019 musical fantasy film featuring an all-star ensemble cast that included James Corden, Dame Judi Dench, Idris Elba, Jennifer Hudson, real-life cat lover Taylor Swift and Rebel Wilson. Based on the 1981 musical *Cats*, which was written by Andrew Lloyd Webber, the story tells the tale of Victoria, a young white cat who finds herself alone on the streets of London in the middle of the night, where she is taken under the wings (so to speak) of the resident alley cats, including the tabby, Jennyanydots. The film may not have done so well at the box office, but the stage version of *Cats* has been presented in over 30 countries and seen by more than 75 million people worldwide. The film version of *Cats* was released digitally on this day in 2020.

Socrate

Socrate is the cat-in-residence at the elegant and iconic Le Bristol hotel in Paris and was the cover star — along with *Emily in Paris* actor Lily Collins — of a super-chic *Harper's Bazaar* online feature celebrating all things related to the Netflix hit which propelled Lily to international fame. The borrowed cat is clearly at home in his luxury surroundings and is such a furball of white hair he probably left his mark on Lily's smart Celine black and white dress. Animal lover Lily, who is the daughter of British rock star and former Genesis band member Phil Collins, was born on this day in Guildford in 1989. Although he no longer has pets, a younger Phil once posted a Valentine's photo of himself cuddling two sibling kittens.

Hamilton the Hipster Cat

Hamilton the hipster cat is an internet celebrity cat with markings that give him a very distinctive white 'moustache'. He has used his platform to raise vast amounts of money for animal charities and his first post on his Instagram account was on this day in 2014. Hamilton's owner is a man called Jay Stowe, based in San Francisco. Jay, who had grown up with cats, knew he wanted a rescue and says that when he visited the local animal shelter, there were just two male kittens – one who was super-friendly, and Hamilton, who cowered in the corner and hissed if anyone went near him. But one of the shelter volunteers picked up the kitten and placed him in Jay's hands, where he promptly fell fast asleep. 'I couldn't leave without him after that,' says Jay.

Pig

In the DreamWorks animated film *Home*, Pig is the calico cat with the corkscrew curly tail (hence the name) who accompanies her owner, a little girl called Gratuity Tucci – nicknamed Tip – on her search for her mum. Earth has been taken over by an alien race called the Boov, and so Pig is Tip's only companion until they join forces with an outcast Boov alien called Oh, who is never sure what to make of Pig's purring and cuddling up. Tip is voiced by the singer Rihanna, and the film, which grossed US$ 386 million worldwide, was released in the UK on this day in 2015.

21 MARCH

Beerbohm, the theatre cat

When Beerbohm, the resident cat at the Globe (now the Gielgud) Theatre, died at the grand old age of 20 on 21 March 1995, actors' newspaper *The Stage* honoured him with a front-page obituary. 'During the course of his career,' it read, 'he overcame a near-fatal road accident in Soho.' In return for his work at the theatre, catching mice, greeting actors in their dressing rooms and waiting for latecomers, Beerbohm had the run of the place – and that included the stage, which he several times strolled across during plays. Perhaps he was a frustrated thespian. He might be the most famous of London's theatre cats but he's not unique. The Bush Theatre in West London has employed a succession of theatre cats over the years, including ex-Battersea residents Marley and Pirate.

22 MARCH

Your Soulmate

According to the Buddhist faith, the body of your cat is the temporary resting place for the soul of a very spiritual being who has lived before you. Some people believe cats spend half their time on Planet Earth with you and the other half astral travelling; they also say if a cat finds its way to you, it will stay with you forever, even after death, because your souls are so deeply bonded. On this day in 1784, the spectacular Emerald Buddha was moved to its current location of Wat Phra Kaew in the grounds of the Grand Palace in Bangkok, Thailand.

23 MARCH

Pickles & Princess Leia

Animal activist and TV presenter Gail Porter has shared just how much she both appreciated and depended on the company of her cat Pickles during lockdown in the UK when she was unable to see any of her family. Gail, who celebrates her birthday today, grew up with a blue half-Persian cat called Princess Leia who lived to the ripe old age of 21, and has often spoken about the positive impact animals can have on people's mental health. She says taking care of black cat Pickles gave her 'a positive focus' every day.

24 MARCH

Wang & Ting

These two sleek Siamese cats lived at one of New York's most prestigious addresses: an apartment above the world-famous Carnegie Hall. They can now be seen in the Hall's digital archive collection of photos that belonged to their owner (and resident) Lisan Kay Nimura, who lived there with her husband, the Japanese dancer and choreographer Yeichi Nimura. He was the 16th generation of a samurai family while she was the daughter of a piano teacher and a reverend. Born Elizabeth Malvina Hathaway in Ohio, she was both Yeichi's wife and his dance partner. Carnegie Hall was funded by Andrew Carnegie of the steel magnate fame. The Carnegie company was formed in New Jersey on this day in 1900.

25 MARCH

Gemmy

Of course, someone as chic as *Sex and the City* star Sarah Jessica Parker, born on this day in 1965, is a cat lover. 'We are all profoundly besotted,' she wrote on Instagram in January 2019 beside a video of longhair tortoiseshell Gemmy drinking in a very ladylike manner by dipping her paw in the water bowl. Three years later, beside a close-up photo of Gemmy's tabby, ginger and white face and green eyes, SJP wrote: 'Fierce love.' She's also praised her cat's talent in front of the camera, writing: 'It just so happens, every location, every type of light, every place she finds herself flatters.'

26 MARCH

Benjamin & Misu

Damon Albarn, co-founder and frontman of bands Blur and Gorillaz, has been a co-parent and cat dad to at least two cats, one called Benjamin and the other called Misu. These two belonged to Damon's ex, former Elastica singer and now retired musician Justine Frischmann, who once told *NME*, the music bible, that her cats were her most 'treasured possessions' because they offer such unconditional love. On this day 2001, Gorillaz released their first album *Gorillaz*, which went on to sell over seven million copies.

27 MARCH

Tarantino's cat

Today marks the birthday of movie director Quentin Tarantino. While cats may not form a central part of the filmmaker's work, it seems they have inspired perhaps his most famous scene: the dance sequence in critically acclaimed film *Pulp Fiction*, in which Uma Thurman and John Travolta show off their moves. Unlikely though it may seem, Tarantino took inspiration for the much-imitated scene from the 1970 Disney film *The Aristocats*. The director told a TV talk show audience that the image he had in mind for the stylish twists performed by Thurman's character was taken straight from a dance scene in the animated classic.

28 MARCH

Mistinguett

Dirk Bogarde, born on this day in 1921, was the heartthrob who became an arthouse actor, but one thing was constant in his life – his love of animals. His childhood cat he rescued from a rubbish tip – then, in the November 1953 issue of *My Home* magazine, a journalist describes his cats on a visit to his Buckinghamshire farmhouse. 'Dirk is very fond of animals and we soon met his other pets,' she writes. 'A Siamese cat, called Mistinguett because she has long black boots, was adopted. The beautiful chinchilla cat was given to Dirk by Sally Ann Howes during the filming of *Quartet*, and named George Bland after the character he was playing.'

29 MARCH

Mitsou

Screen siren Marilyn Monroe adored animals and owned a white Persian cat called Mitsou. The actress starred in the wonderful comedy film *Some Like It Hot*, which was released on this day in 1959 and also starred Tony Curtis and Jack Lemmon, whose characters passed themselves off as members of an all-female jazz band to hide from the Mafia after they witness a murder. Speaking of her love of animals, Marilyn, who often felt she wasn't taken seriously as an actor, famously said, 'If you talk to a dog or cat, it doesn't tell you to shut up.'

Scarlett

They say there is nothing more powerful than a mother's love for her offspring — and this little rescue cat proved that in spades when she braved a burning blaze to get her kittens to safety, one by one. Scarlett was a stray and sheltering in a New York garage when the fire broke out on this day in 1996. Once the firefighters had the blaze under control, they noticed the young cat ferrying her kittens to safety, despite getting badly burned each time she went back into the garage to do so. The firefighters raced Scarlett and her litter to a local veterinary surgeon. Scarlett's bravery struck such a chord with cat lovers that over 7,000 people came forward to rehome her. Eventually, she went to a cat lover called Karen Wellen, who had written to say she was only interested in offering a home to animals with special needs. Soon after, an animal award for heroism was created in Scarlett's name.

31 MARCH

Smudge

'Sister Smudge (*c.* 1970–2000) was a much-loved employee of the People's Palace and the only cat to be a full member of the GMB Union' reads an intriguing plaque at one of the entrances to Glasgow's People's Palace museum. Pretty black and white Smudge was brought into the palace for her skills as a rodent-catcher but soon became a Glasgow celebrity with ceramic sculptures of her selling out in the museum shop. The GMB union, which today represents around 500,000 workers across all industries, was created by the merger of several unions, including the National Union of Gas Workers and General Labourers, which was founded on this day in 1889 by Will Thorne with the support of Eleanor Marx, Karl Marx's daughter. A cat lover, Eleanor would surely have delighted in Smudge's membership.

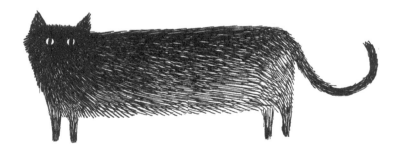

APRIL

1 APRIL

All cats, large and small

On this day in 1973, the Indian government launched the pioneering Project Tiger to promote conservation and stop wildlife crime – so today we celebrate cats great and small. All cats belong to the Felidae family of mammals, with all modern-day cats – from tigers to pet cats – descending from the oldest cat lineage, the *Panthera* line. This means that the domestic cat shares 95.6 per cent of its DNA with a tiger! And that's not where the similarities end: just like a tiger, your cat will scent-mark its territory, need to eat meat, enjoy alone time and love a sheltered space to chill out.

2 APRIL

Nyan Cat

Nyan Cat, who is also known as Pop Tart Cat, is an award-winning GIF of an animated cat who has the body – yes, you've guessed it – of a pop tart flying through space.

The original GIF was posted on this day 2011. Three days later, the GIF was uploaded to YouTube with a now-famous backing track. And in 2012 Nyan cat won 'Meme of the Year' at the Webby Awards. Even more extraordinary, in 2021, the meme sold as an NFT for 300 ETH (Ethereum) which was worth an estimated $590,000 at the time. It was the first meme to be sold as an NFT, leading to Nyan Cat's creator telling the world, 'Basically, I've opened the door to a whole new meme economy in the crypto world.'

3 APRIL

Vito's cat

There was no cat written into the original script for the film *The Godfather*, but when the director, Francis Ford Coppola, spotted a stray cat lurking near the set at the Paramount lot he picked him up and handed him to Marlon Brando, who was playing the fictional Mafia boss Vito Corleone. The grey striped tabby settled into Brando's lap for an iconic scene, and films buffs have said ever since that the little cat served to underscore Vito's soft and unassuming exterior but also to remind us that all cats have hidden claws! Marlon Brando was born on this day in 1924.

4 APRIL

Cat King

The Memphis Flash, Elvis the Pelvis, or simply The King; Elvis Presley has many names, but his fanbase in China knows him by an altogether more feline moniker: Cat King. A uniquely Chinese nickname, pronounced as something close to 'mao-wang', its origin is uncertain, but some believe it relates to the old and not widely used label of Elvis as 'the Hillbilly Cat', which seems to have caught on in China. The Hillbilly Cat was later used as the name of a compliation album of Elvis' songs, but it's only in China that the King is known as Cat King. It was on this day in 1960 that Elvis recorded his version of the song 'Are You Lonesome Tonight?'.

5 APRIL

Swinburne's Cat

The poet Algernon Charles Swinburne, born on this day in 1837, was surely a lover of cats, addressing one in his poem 'To a Cat' as a 'stately, kindly, lordly friend' and imploring it to 'condescend' to sit next to him. Another poet, Christopher Smart, elevated his cat to an even higher status, describing Jeoffry as 'the servant of the Living God' and imbuing him with a virtuous spirit bordering on the divine. 'For he purrs in thankfulness, when God tells him he's a good Cat,' Smart writes. Irish poet W.B. Yeats, meanwhile, imagined a moon-worshipping cat dancing under the lunar light: 'Minnaloushe runs in the grass / Lifting his delicate feet. / Do you dance, Minnaloushe, do you dance?'

6 APRIL

Monsieur & Ramona

The British-born surrealist painter and novelist Leonora Carrington, who lived most of her adult life in Mexico City, had a cat-like spirit, conducting herself with confidence and an air of independence. A founding member of the women's liberation movement in Mexico in the 1970s, she was born to a wealthy textile manufacturer and into a Roman Catholic family, but rebelled from an early age and was expelled from two schools. It's perhaps not surprising that Leonora, who was born on this day in 1917, embodied feline defiance: she owned a pair of Siamese cats, Monsieur and Ramona, and was besotted with them, often being photographed holding them and even incorporating cats into her artworks, not least in the 1952 painting titled *Cats*.

7 APRIL

Nala

Nala Cat – who is the most followed cat on Instagram – released her book *Living Your Best Life According to Nala Cat* on this day in 2020. Nala was awarded her Guinness World Record for the most Instagram followers for a cat in 2020. At the time of writing, her follower count stands at a whopping 4.5 million! The Siamese/tabby mix was adopted from a rescue in the United States by her owner, Verasiri Methachittipan, and subsequently captured the adoration of the internet with her wide blue eyes and super-cute habit of curling up into cardboard boxes.

8 APRIL

Blofeld's cat

Ian Fleming's book *From Russia with Love* was published on this day in 1957, but it was missing an icon who was to pop up in the screen version – a white Persian cat who sits, inscrutable, on the villain Blofeld's lap. The cat, who has appeared in several films since, has never been named but has become as famous as his owner and – the true stamp of a star – much parodied, including in the Austin Powers films. Several cats have played the role over the years.

9 APRIL

The first pet cat

Could this be the world's first pet cat? On this date in 2004, cat lovers across the world were reading research by a team of archaeologists about a recent dig in Cyprus which shattered all previous theories about how long cats had been cherished as pets. Until then it had been assumed that the first cat who crossed the threshold to become a pet belonged to an Ancient Egyptian family, around 3,500 years ago. But a grave excavated in Cyprus revealed the bones of a man and his cat, buried just 40cm (15 inches) apart and more than 9,000 years old.

10 APRIL

Timmy, Tommy, Foxy & Frankie

British Modernist artist Ben Nicholson (1894–1982) was a huge lover of cats and often incorporated them into his work. He was born on this day in 1894. Tate in London has a large selection of photos of him holding various cats, including Timmy, Tommy, Foxy and Frankie. In 1933, he even painted (abstract of course) Frankie and Foxy, and while to the non-art connoisseur that black and white line image might look a little bit like two triangles with one eye each, rest assured this is a painterly interpretation of a cat!

11 APRIL

Charles Baudelaire

'*Chat mystérieux, / Chat séraphique, chat étrange*' – French writer Charles Baudelaire, born this week in Paris in 1821, was fascinated by the mysterious and angelic character of the cat. Indeed, he was once himself described, by his friend and fellow cat lover Théophile Gautier, as a 'voluptuous wheedling cat with velvety manners'. In his celebrated poem *'Le Chat'*, he implores: 'Come, my fine cat, against my loving heart; / Sheathe your sharp claws, and settle. / And let my eyes into your pupils dart, / Where agate sparks with metal.' In his time, Baudelaire was considered an eccentric by many, an impression only furthered by his custom of entering a house and extravagantly introducing himself to the feline occupants before the humans.

Yo-Yo & Mac

American film actor and director Mel Gibson makes no secret of his love of cats and recently posted an older photograph of himself on Facebook with a little black kitten, likely to be a young Yo-Yo. In his 1993 film *The Man Without a Face*, Mel plays a disfigured recluse who has a cat called Mac, but perhaps his most iconic film role to date is as the eponymous hero of *Mad Max*, which was first released in Australia, where it was filmed, on this day in 1979.

Garry

Chess grandmaster Garry Kasparov, born on this day in 1963, is said to have an IQ of 135. It's a shame a namesake cat in Hove, Sussex wasn't born quite so bright. Garry's owners were distraught when, at an annual check-up in March 2015, the vet felt a mass in his stomach. An X-ray confirmed a suspected tumour. Next day, with Garry in surgery to remove it, Ana steeled herself for the worst. But, picking Garry up from the vets after his surgery, Ana was handed a plastic bag containing Garry's tumour — two shoelaces and a dozen hair bands. 'I had washed some laces from my trainers which went missing but I never for one moment thought Garry was the reason why,' Ana gasped. Garry survived with just a scar and Ana now buys chunky clips instead of rubber bands for her hair.

14 APRIL

Governor Grey

Governor Grey is a clever Burmese cat who took up residence in Old Government House in the Auckland University City Campus after turning up as a stray. The cat wanders freely around the campus and, if he feels like it, attends poetry readings, meetings and lectures. He likes to eat off antique china plates and is a firm favourite with students, lecturers and visitors alike, although his official owner now is college custodian Emma Newborn, who adopted him after no previous owner could be traced. Governor Grey is named after former New Zealand Prime Minister Sir George Grey, who was born on this day 1812.

15 APRIL

Cat's Eyes

Cats have good night vision – although they can't see in the dark without any light available. Their eyes are very sensitive to movement, however, and they have excellent peripheral vision. So it's perhaps no surprise that they gave their name to the reflective cat's eyes you see in the middle of the road, which were invented by Percy Shaw, an inventor who was born in Yorkshire on this day in 1890. Percy had been struggling to drive home in the fog one night when his headlights caught the gleam of the eyes of a cat who was sitting on the fence . . . and the rest, as they say, is history.

Sarah Snow

'Cats are only human, they have their faults,' the writer Kingsley Amis, born on this day in 1922, said. He shared his London home with a cat called Sarah Snow, perhaps so-named in recognition of her long-ish white fur, and wrote poems about her, including one for a poetry anthology for children in which he sweetly reports Sarah's attempts to learn English.

Balerion

Balerion was a kitten who belonged to Princess Rhaenys Targaryen in the hit HBO TV series *Game of Thrones*. The Princess likes to pretend the little black cat – who was named after the great dragon Balerion, the Black Dread – was a real dragon. The cat's namesake was remembered for having been the largest dragon who ever existed. He eventually died of old age and his massive skull, which we see in the series premier, was kept by the Targaryens in the Red Keep. *Game of Thrones*, which ran for eight seasons and ended in 2019, first premiered on this day in 2011.

18 APRIL

Lil Bub

Lil Bub was one of the original American online celebrity cats, known for her unique appearance. Originally gaining fame on the internet, she was the subject of the documentary *Lil Bub & Friendz*, which premiered at the Tribeca Film Festival on this day in 2013. The documentary also features other internet cats such as Grumpy Cat, Keyboard Cat and Nyan Cat. Lil Bub was originally found as the runt of a healthy feral litter living in a tool shed in rural Indiana in the summer of 2011. She was taken in as a rescue who needed special care and overcame many health challenges to live a happy life until her death in 2019. To date, Lil Bub's Big Fund has raised $500,000 for animals in need, a wonderful legacy.

19 APRIL

Zelda & Sammy

Bookworm actor James Franco, who celebrates his birthday today, names all of his cats after characters in books. Zelda is named after the wife of novelist F. Scott Fitzgerald, who wrote *The Great Gatsby*, and Sammy is named after Sammy Glick from Budd Schulberg's book *What Makes Sammy Run?*. James' brother Dave is also a cat lover and, according to James, stole two of his cats – Harry and Arturo – from his actor sibling. Harry was named after Harry Angstrom from John Updike's *Rabbit* novels and Arturo was named after Arturo Bandini from the John Fante novels.

20 APRIL

Buster

A clever rescue cat on the Scottish island of Bute put paw to paper on this day in 2020, publishing, with a little help from his owner Denise Marinucci, his biography – and a tearjerker it is too. A year later, Buster and Denise published: *Buster's Cat Pawetry: A Photo Book o' Scottish Feline Verse.* In one poem, Buster asks his readers not to overlook older cats in shelters. 'An older cat's faithful an true, he knows what he's wanting fae you,' Buster writes, 'No infantile silliness, crazed willynillyness, jes tha full royal treatment will do!'

21 APRIL

Minou and Puss

A cat at Scotney Castle in Kent is up to mischief, dangling its paw over the side of a fountain in an attempt to hook a fish. The fish need not fear, though – the cat is made of stone, commissioned by cat lover Betty Hussey, mistress of Scotney, as a 90th birthday present to herself. Betty owned a succession of Burmese called Minou – one of whom the fountain cat is modelled on – but, at the time of her death, aged 99 on this day in 2006, her feline companion was a tortoiseshell named Puss. When the National Trust took over the running of Scotney, Puss stayed put, napping on Betty's bed. But, even though she was adored by all, a few modifications did have to be made to her luxury lifestyle, including eating tinned cat food instead of fresh salmon for dinner.

22 APRIL

Gobbolino

Gobbolino the kitten does not want to be a witch's cat, the role into which he's been born. His sister Sootica is excited to follow in their mother's paw-steps and climb aboard a witch's broom, but not Gobbolino. 'I want to be good and have people love me,' explains the eponymous hero of the classic children's novel by Ursula Moray Williams, born this week in 1911, says. 'People don't love witches' cats. They are too disagreeable.' So, while Sootica is apprenticed to a witch, Gobbolino tries to forge his own path. But – with his one white paw and blue eyes, he doesn't even look like a kitchen cat. Nor does he know how to behave like a normal cat, making blue sparks come out of his whiskers to amuse children and inviting hobgoblins into the house. He's turned out of every kitchen he tries to make home until Sootica puts a spell on him, transforming him into a kitchen cat by nature as well as inclination. His coat turns tabby and all the magic leaves his body but, at last, he's content. 'While there's a fire on the hearth, there's a place beside it for you,' the farmer and his wife tell him.

23 APRIL

Raminou

Every bit an artist's muse, ginger Raminou was the much-loved cat of Suzanne Valadon, an exhibition of whose work was just beginning at Centre Pompidou-Metz, north-east France, on this day in 2023. Valadon, born in 1865, learned the tricks of the artist's trade through working as a model for painters including Toulouse-Lautrec and became known for female nudes on which she offered a fresh, woman-to-woman perspective, portraying strength and independence. Valadon painted many pictures of Raminou, often resplendent on cloths of different shades.

24 APRIL

Jinx

On this day in 2022, black cat Jinx became the first pet mayor of Hell, a small town just outside Ann Arbor, Michigan, which offers a Mayor of the Day package for $100. But Jinx, who had been rescued as a kitten and who at the time had over 400,000 Instagram followers, is not the only pet to stray into politics. She followed in the footsteps of Stubbs, a strawberry blonde cat who was Mayor of Talkeetna not for a day but for a staggering 19 years. Stubbs stayed in post until his death in 2016 and worked to keep taxes down for the town's 900 two-legged population.

25 APRIL

Dave's Cats

English indie band Blur released their classic album *Parklife* on this day in 1994, but it's more a case of Farmlife for drummer Dave Rowntree's three cats, who share his Surrey farmhouse with his dog, two sheep and a horse. 'That's the benefit of not living in London – you can have a menagerie,' Rowntree told the *Evening Standard* in 2023. Dave's trio of felines includes a stray black cat who just rocked up one day, obviously fancying living in a house, a very big house in the country.

Vienna

Rising Damp was one of the most popular sitcoms of the 1970s, starring Leonard Rossiter as the grumpy, misanthropic bedsit landlord Rupert Rigsby, desperately in love with one of his unfortunate tenants Miss Jones. Rigsby's cat Vienna is forced to listen to many of his grumbles – indeed, he's often the subject of them. But, in an episode called 'Clunk Click', first broadcast on this day in 1977, Rigsby takes Miss Jones for a rather exuberant spin in his sports car and then, after parking up, spots something furry beneath the wheels. 'Oh Vienna . . . oh my little boy,' he wails. 'Funny to think he'll never creep up on my lap and sink his claws into my thighs anymore.' Rigsby and Miss Jones hold a funeral service for Vienna, singing the hymn 'Rock of Ages'. Then another boarder, Alan, walks in with Vienna, right as rain, in his arms. So what's Rigsby just cremated? Miss Jones' Aunt Ada's fur stole!

27 APRIL

Gli

Visitors to the Hagia Sophia in Istanbul were delighted by the presence of Gli, a pretty, tabby cat who added a sense of peace and contentment to the Mosque. She even greeted Barack Obama when he visited in 2009 and was rewarded with a presidential pat. Gli was born at the Hagia Sophia in 2004 and made it her home, stretching out on the cool marble floors on hot days and getting comfy among the cushions in winter. On this date in 2019, her Instagram page featured her having a good old yawn. Sadly Gli died in November 2020 after a short illness but her Instagram page remains, featuring images of all the magnificent cats of Istanbul.

Charlie

In times of trouble, cats usually step up to the plate, providing companionship and comfort to their families through a stressful or lonely time. Prior to lockdown in spring 2020, Charlie, a black and white cat from Camberwell, south-east London, spent most of his time out and about, proving his status as top cat of the street. But that spring, he became a home boy, preferring to stay in with owner June. 'I worried I'd be lonely, maybe grow depressed,' June, 70 and single, remembers. 'But Charlie wasn't having that. Mornings he woke me at 8 a.m. prompt for breakfast – then he demanded I wave around a stick with a fluffy mouse on the end for him. Time for elevenses...and then he'd supervise me as I made lunch. His companionship meant a lot. It was just having another living being in the flat, someone to natter to.'

Mr Bigglesworth

If you're an Austin Powers fan, then Mr Bigglesworth (played by brilliantly named cat actor Ted Nude-Gent) probably needs no introduction because he's the cat that belongs to Dr. Evil in the spy parody film which premiered on this day in 1997. It is said that filming of the hit film was delayed more than once because of Ted's penchant for snoozing peacefully on star Mike Myers's lap between takes. Ted is a Sphynx cat who belongs to a Hollywood trainer.

Tabby cats

In 2016 this date was chosen as National Tabby Day in the United States. Tabbies have a characteristic letter 'M' on their foreheads, a mark that has been ascribed different meanings and origins depending on different cultures. Celtic legend tells of a story of the tabby being granted the latter after an act of kindness, while some believe that it relates to the word *mau*, the word used for cats in ancient Egypt.

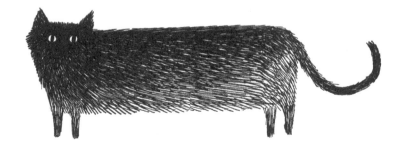

MAY

1 MAY

Stewie

The longest cat ever recorded was a Maine Coon called Mymains Steward Gilligan (or Stewie, for short). Stewie, who was from Nevada, USA, stretched out a staggering 123cm (48 inches). Originally called Dylan, he joined his forever family on this day in 2005. He was always getting under his owner's feet, so they named him after Stewie, the toddler in the animated TV series *Family Guy*. A cat's spine is super flexible – because cats have 53 loosely fitting vertebrae, around 20 more than a human. A cat can jump up to six times its own length.

2 MAY

Bagel

Actor and writer Kumail Nanjiani, who played Kingo in the Marvel superhero film *Eternals* (2021), likes to read to his cat Bagel. The acting life clearly doesn't extend to Bagel; Kumail says his cat could never last an entire day on a film set because she likes sleeping so much! In *Eternals*, Kingo is a superhero disguised on earth as a Bollywood actor. The film also featured a cat called Goose (*see* 18 October for more on the four gorgeous cats who played that role). Kumail who is also known for *The Big Sick* (2017) and was born in Karachi, Sindh, Pakistan, on this day in 1978.

3 MAY

Gumball

Gumball Watterson is a 12-year-old blue cat and star of the animated sitcom *The Amazing World of Gumball*. The show, which also features Gumball's adoptive goldfish brother and best friend, Darwin, was first shown on this day 2011 on the Cartoon Network. Gumball and Darwin live in the fictional American city of Elmore with his clever sister, Anais, and stay-at-home dad, Richard (both of whom are rabbits) and his workaholic mom, Nicole, who is another cat. The show aired 240 episodes over six seasons and ran until 2019.

4 MAY

Stapledon

Tuxedo cat Stapledon, named after Walter de Stapledon, the Bishop of Exeter over 700 years ago, is the latest in a long line of resident cats at Exeter Cathedral. Stapledon is often spotted poking his head out of the hole in the Cathedral door created for the cats of the fifteenth century, who were paid a penny a week to keep the building mice-free. Exeter Cathedral, founded in 1050, is one of the grandest in England, but it was bombed in the early hours of the morning of 4 May 1942 and debris from the mediaeval chapel scattered far and wide. Tom the Cathedral cat survived, only to be attacked by an owl during a fracas over a rat, losing an eye. In his honour, sculptors created a carving of a one-eyed cat as they rebuilt the chapel. Hopefully Stapledon will avoid any tussles with owls. Meantime, as he tells readers of his blog, he's enjoying the freedom of the Cathedral: 'As the official cat there are many places that I can get to that members of the public can't.'

5 MAY

Mr Barnes

The Scottish writer Sir Compton Mackenzie wrote *Whisky Galore* in 1947, subsequently made into two films – one in 1949 and one released on this day in Scotland in 2016. Sir Mackenzie's life could have been called Siamese Cats Galore because he adored the breed, serving for many years as President of the Siamese Cat Club of Great Britain. In the first of several volumes of his autobiography, Mackenzie remembers a childhood cat called Mr Barnes. 'Mr Barnes accompanied me everywhere and liked to rest with me during that hour when the two-year-old was supposed to recover from the exhaustion of the morning and be ready to eat his dinner,' he wrote. 'Nanny had a ludicrous notion that by resting with me Mr Barnes would draw my breath and so he was always hustled away. However, to my relief he nearly always managed to get back . . . and how grateful I was when two black beetles appeared beside my cot and were chased away by Mr Barnes.'

6 MAY

Queen Camilla

On this day in 2023, Their Majesties King Charles and Queen Camilla were crowned at Westminster Abbey. HM The Queen is Battersea's Royal Patron and honoured the two dogs she rehomed from Battersea, Beth and Bluebell, with their images embroidered in gold on her Coronation gown. 'Along I went to Battersea, and Beth appeared, and she had just been moved from pillar to post and dumped,' Camilla said in an interview, explaining her adoption of the duo. 'We thought it would be nice for her to have a friend. They found Bluebell two or three weeks later, wandering about in the woods, no hair on her, covered in sores, virtually dead. And they nursed her back to life and her hair grew again. She's very sweet, but a tiny bit neurotic, shall we say.' It's not all about the dogs, though – Camilla opened Battersea's new state-of-the-art cattery in 2010 and enjoyed a cuddle with a tabby kitten.

Monty

Ginger tabby Monty came to fame after saving his owner's life. Patricia Peter had only recently been diagnosed as diabetic when she was woken in the middle of the night in March 2011 by Monty repeatedly nibbling the fingers of her left hand. Monty had no history of biting and bizarrely was only bothering the hand that Patricia would use to test her blood sugar levels. Patricia, who was feeling weak and dizzy, decided to test her levels and sure enough, the reading was low enough to cause serious risk. She treated herself and noticed how Monty stayed glued to her side, keeping her awake until her levels returned to normal. On this day the following year (2012), Monty was inducted into an animal Hall of Fame to commemorate his heroic actions.

Coraline's Black Cat

When Coraline Jones moves home with her writer parents, who are always too busy to spend time with her, she discovers a hidden door in their new house which leads to a more fun-filled world than the one where she lives. She also finds a black cat who can talk. The Cat (voiced by Keith David) plays a pivotal role in helping Coraline defeat the scary character known as The Other Mother. The film, based on the novella by British writer Neil Gaiman, was released in the United Kingdom on this day in 2009.

9 MAY

The Piano Man Cat Rooms

Cat-loving singer-songwriter Billy Joel performed his 70th birthday show in Madison Square Gardens on this day in 2019 and afterwards donated all proceeds to help fund two cat rooms at a local animal shelter. The two rooms are called the Piano Man rooms and are designed to make all the rescue cats and kittens that play there feel safe and cared for. The 'Uptown Girl' and 'Piano Man' hit-maker, who is worth an estimated $225 million, is a huge animal advocate; his own pets are all rescues.

Pepper

Hollywood is full of rags-to-riches stories, but few are as dramatic as that of Pepper, one of the first cats to grace the silver screen. Legend has it that Pepper, a stray grey cat, popped up from under the floorboards in the middle of filming at Keystone Studios in 1912 – and a star was born. Pepper went on to 'act' in many films of the era, including *A Little Hero*, released this week in 1913 in the United States, for which she received her first namecheck on the credits. She worked with Charlie Chaplin and the Keystone Cops, but her favourite co-star was Teddy the Great Dane and, the pair, who played a funny and poignant little and large act, became great friends. At the height of her fame Pepper was insured for US$ 5,000 – a fortune back then. But, when Teddy died, she refused to appear with any other dogs.

11 MAY

George

Ginger George is the station cat at Stourbridge Junction in the West Midlands and, as well as cheering up visitors and staff, the sweet-natured feline is spreading love over social media with inspiring messages. 'No matter how bad things may feel right now, I promise you that you won't feel this way forever,' he wrote on 11 May 2023. Every morning George arrives from his nearby home for work where he's busy sitting on top of the ticket office filing cabinet keeping an eye on things, rummaging in his big cardboard treat box, performing yoga stretches and napping in his fluffy doughnut bed. When Stourbridge Junction was named Britain's favourite train station in 2021, George's social media fans were credited with contributing, in large part, to the win.

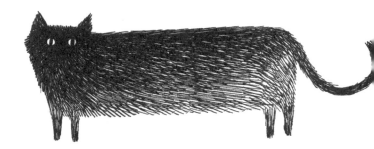

12 MAY

Mr White

The Lady with the Lamp, Florence Nightingale, born on this day in 1820, was also very much a cat lady, cherishing 60 furry companions through her lifetime. During the Crimean War she'd appreciated the cat's skills in killing disease-spreading rats and, back in Britain, repaid feline-kind with a life of luxury. When her cats had kittens, she scrupulously vetted potential owners and in a letter to someone adopting the 'most affectionate and intelligent' Mr White, a ten-month old Angora tom, she lists his peccadillos, which must be indulged, writing: 'He has always been used to having his meals by himself like a gentleman on a plate.'

13 MAY

Gia Marie

The creator of the HBO hit series *Girls*, Lena Dunham celebrates her birthday today. She has a portrait of the head of a rescue Sphynx cat called Gia Marie tattooed on her left shoulder. Sadly, Gia, who had a previous heart condition, passed away in 2018, but the Golden Globe-winning American writer, actor and producer has gone on to rescue other cats and often includes photos of them in the stories she shares with her three million Instagram followers. Lena says she does not shy away from offering a home to rescue pets with life-limiting conditions and actually prefers to adopt older animals from rescue shelters.

14 MAY

Warwick

Cate Blanchett, born on this day in 1969, has admitted she's actually more of a dog than a cat person but says her Tonkinese Warwick, named by her kids, was more canine than feline anyway. 'I treated Warwick like a dog,' the double Oscar winner explained. 'I just thought: I'm not really a cat person. I put that out there to Warwick and he started behaving like a dog. We go for a walk down the garden or down the lane and he will walk with us. He thinks he's a Labrador – no, he's a cat. Shush, don't tell him.'

15 MAY

Fanchette & Petiteu

'Time spent with a cat is never wasted.' So said the French writer Sidonie-Gabrielle Colette, famous enough to be known by just her surname. Colette spent her life in the company of cats, dogs and three husbands. Her novella *Gigi* was turned into a 1958 film starring Leslie Caron and Maurice Chevalier, released on this day in 1958, and winning nine gongs at the 1959 Oscars – a record not surpassed until 2004. Colette's works were sensual, rather like cats – indeed, her short novel *La Chatte* is a tale of a man who cares for his cat more than he ever could for any woman. Colette herself was photographed several times with her Chartreux cats, whom she gifted fanciful names like Fanchette and Petiteu, overseeing her while she wrote.

16 MAY

Hodge

In his biography of Samuel Johnson, published on this date in 1791, James Boswell wrote of the famous poet, playwright, essayist and dictionary compiler: 'I never shall forget the indulgence with which he treated Hodge, his cat: for whom he himself used to go out and buy oysters.' Hodge, a black cat, is now immortalised in bronze outside Johnson's former home on Gough Square, just off London's Fleet Street, sitting on a dictionary with a rather grumpy expression on his face and the inscription 'a very fine cat indeed'. The statue also features a pair of empty oyster shells; his luxury lifestyle is being maintained. Although cats eating oysters is definitely not something we recommend!

17 MAY

Le Chat Noir

Le Chat Noir – which translates to The Black Cat – was a nineteenth-century cabaret (probably the world's first) in the fashionably bohemian district of Montmartre, Paris. A favourite haunt of writers, artists and composers, it is also the place where the classical pianist and composer Erik Satie first made his name. Satie, who wrote the haunting and now famous *Gymnopédies* series, was employed as a second pianist at the nightclub, accompanying the singers and also playing the background music for the popular shadow plays in the upstairs theatre where cut-out figures were used to cast 'shadows' on the backlit walls for storytelling. The composer, whose father was French and whose mother was British, was born on this day in 1866.

18 MAY

Unsinkable Sam

The clue to this uplifting tale lies in the cat's name. Nobody knows his original name, but he was called Oscar (or Oskar) by the sailors who rescued him from the sea after the ship he had been on sank. (In the International Code of Signals, 'O' is code for 'Man Overboard'.) British sailors on HMS *Cossack* spotted the black and white cat perched on a piece of wood and brought him to safety on board their ship. Oscar earned his nickname, Unsinkable Sam, because he survived not only the *Bismarck* going down, but also two further sinkings: first HMS *Cossack* and then HMS *Ark Royal*. The *Bismarck* first set sail with Oscar on board on this day in 1941. Sam retired after that last sinking and lived out his days in a home for retired sailors in Belfast.

19 MAY

Yang

Caring cat Yang is the mascot of Hexham Hospital where, for the past six years, he has adopted the role of meeter and greeter for staff, patients and visitors, a role that became even more important during the COVID-19 pandemic. On this day in 2023, ginger Yang was awarded a key to the town of Hexham by local councillors in honour of his service – along with, perhaps of more interest to him, a bag of cat treats. 'Yang has this sixth sense for people who need him,' owner Glynis Bell said. 'A paramedic told me that he peers into the ambulance if a patient has just arrived and, however frightened they are, his big ginger face makes them smile.'

20 MAY

Think Think & Ah Tsai

Tsai Ing-wen, the cat-loving first female president of Taiwan, started her presidential term on this day in 2016. She currently has two cats, Think Think and Ah Tsai, who have appeared alongside her throughout her campaigns and are often brought along to events. Think Think is a female grey tabby and Ah Tsai is a ginger male tabby. Tsai Ing-wen was re-elected in 2020 with the highest number of votes in the history of Taiwan's presidential elections.

21 MAY

Brody

When comedian Sarah Millican appeared on *Room 101*, one of her pet – literally – hates was cats that ignore her. Luckily for her she has no such problems with her own cat Brody, named after the police chief in *Jaws*. In March 2020 she announced on Facebook that, after nearly a decade, Brody had finally decided to sit on her lap. 'Heaven for the five minutes he stays,' she wrote. Ginger Brody has often been the subject of her stand-up routines. On her Home Bird stand-up tour, which opened on her home turf in Newcastle on this date in 2014, she described Brodie first arriving at her flat and having a snoop around. 'He went round the back of the sofa and I was surprised because I've never been round the back of the sofa and the Hoover certainly hasn't,' she said. 'And he came back round with what can only be described as four big grey fluffy slippers on.'

22 MAY

Calvin

This week in 1870, American essayist and newspaperman Charles Dudley Warner was tending to the garden of his Connecticut farmhouse, hoeing the corn while observed by his horticultural helpmate, Calvin the cat. Warner wrote a series of essays on gardening for the local newspaper – then published them as a book, *My Summer in a Garden*. Calvin, according to Warner, was a cat of 'uncommon character' who possessed 'qualities worthy of imitation', and was also a keen gardener. 'He delighted, above all things, to accompany me walking about the garden, hearing the birds, getting the smell of the fresh earth, and rejoicing in the sunshine,' Warner wrote. 'If I worked, he sat and watched me, or looked off over the bank, and kept his ear open to the twitter in the cherry-trees.'

Melvin

Vets in Glasgow were very confused on this day in 2023 when they checked a stray cat's microchip – and discovered he was registered to an address in Australia! An animal inspector had collected the silver tabby after locals in Renfrewshire, who'd been feeding him since Christmas, grew concerned for his well-being. The mystery was soon solved, however. Melvin, as the cat was called, was indeed an Aussie cat but, in summer 2022, had moved to Scotland with his family. Just eight weeks later, Melvin disappeared. 'We were devastated when Melvin went missing,' owner Jacqueline Dick explained. 'We did everything we could think of to try and find him, but by winter we feared the worst. The first night we got him home he didn't leave my side and was purring really loudly.'

24 MAY

Star Trek Cats

The mission of those aboard the Starship Enterprise is to 'seek out new life and new civilisations' – but perhaps they didn't need to look much further than their own ship to find some unexpected life forms. At least that's the case in the book *Star Trek Cats*, a loving homage to the long-running sci-fi franchise that re-imagines the adventures of Captain Kirk, Spock and their cast of allies and enemies with a twist: everyone involved is, surprise surprise, a cat. Filled with imaginitive illustrations, the book is billed as the perfect gift for fans who can't get enough of science fiction, felines and any combination of the two. On this day in 1993 the Star Trek episode 'Second Chances' aired, guest-starring Mae Jemison, the first time a real-life astronaut appeared on the show.

25 MAY

Bootsy

On this date in 2020, Bootsy the stray ginger and white kitten was getting his paws under the table of Canadian folk legend Joni Mitchell's home after turning up at her gate out of the blue at midnight a week earlier. The day after Bootsy's arrival, Mitchell told a journalist that she'd been lying in bed thinking about getting a cat, only to hear Bootsy's meow. 'I hope nobody comes to claim him,' she confided to the interviewer. Nobody did. Clever Bootsy, choosing to lay his hat at the home of a woman well-known for her love of cats since the 1960s! And he didn't even have to catch a Big Yellow Taxi to get there.

26 MAY

Bobbi

When Janet Llewellyn from Cardiff adopted Bobbi, the grey and white rescue kitten, her 14-year-old collie Shadow was unimpressed, stalking off grumpily whenever the newcomer approached. But, on this date in 2023, a few months after Janet had adopted Bobbi, she returned home from work to find him on top of the cupboard where she kept Shadow's treats – and the treats, their packets ripped open, scattered all over the floor. In the middle of it all was Shadow, licking his lips contentedly. Since then, kitten and old-timer have been the best of friends, playing together and even snoozing curled up in a canine-feline ball.

27 MAY

Delmore

In 1960, American short story writer John Cheever found himself, reluctantly, in charge of a cat, thrust into his arms by a visiting friend who explained she could not keep him. In a letter to her written three years later Cheever, born on this day in 1912, describes his relationship with the cat, now renamed Delmore. There had been some friction and Delmore's misdeeds included relieving himself in a box of tissues. But, ultimately, Cheever had grown fond of the cat, writing: 'Delmore contributes a dynamic to all our relationships. People who dislike me go directly to his side and he is, thus, a peacemaker. He loves to play with toilet paper. He does not like catnip mice . . . he has his role and we all respect it.'

28 MAY

Ron, Pip, Zelda & Tiger

'I am utterly in thrall to the beauty of cats,' writer and comedian David Baddiel said in an interview with the *Guardian* in March 2022. Baddiel, born on this day in 1964, was raised with cats in his childhood home in northwest London, smuggled a stray into his university halls of residence and shared a cat with flatmate Frank Skinner in the 1990s. His current feline companions are ginger, seven-toed Ron; Ron's mother Pip who can be 'lazy and irritable'; 'neat and complex' ginger tabby and white Zelda and Tiger who wants to tap people on the arm but sometimes stops, halfway, 'and so just stays with his paw poised in the air staring at you in hope and confusion'.

29 MAY

Tom Kitten

John F. Kennedy, born on this day in 1917, was a well-known dog lover, turning to them for companionship in times of trouble. But a cat was also resident at the White House during his tenure – his daughter Caroline's Tom Kitten, the first White House cat for half a century. When Tom Kitten died his obituary reported: 'Unlike many humans in the same position, he never wrote his memoirs of his days in the White House and never discussed them for quotation.'

30 MAY

Sammy

The Archers was first broadcast as a five-part pilot, an episode an evening, this week in 1950 and, though the main animal stars in a farming village are the cows and sheep, cats have had their moments. Peggy Archer's cat Sammy, who debuted on the show as a kitten in June 1983, was pivotal to many plot lines. He went missing in a fire at Peggy's cottage in December 1983 – then, in a roundabout way, led her to love. When one suitor Godfrey Wendover laughed at her idea of taking Sammy to a cat show, Jack Woolley offered to accompany her instead. Sammy's success or otherwise at the show is lost in the mists of time but Jack, who took Peggy to dinner after the show, proposed to her a year later. Sammy lived a long and happy life and is now buried near Ambridge golf course next to Jack's beloved dog Captain.

31 MAY

Larry, Matilda (Tildy), Lady G, Liza Meownelli, Baby G & Baggy

So, on this special day we bring you not just one or two but six (!) happy cats, who all belong to the cat-mad American TV star and hair stylist Jonathan Van Ness (JVN), who refers to his cat tribe as his feline family. JVN says Larry is the cuddliest; Liza is actually a boy but when adopted everyone thought 'he was a she'; Matilda likes lots of kisses (but only on her terms of course); and little Baby G is the shy one. On this day in 2023, the TV personality brought his live show to Brighton to kick off his first UK-wide tour.

JUNE

1 JUNE

Rosie

A Norwich cat was celebrating a big birthday today in 2023 – a very big birthday as Rosie the longhair tortoiseshell turned 32. Rosie, who has only been to the vet twice since being born in 1991, now spends her days napping and eating her favourite tinned salmon but she celebrated her big day with a fish cake and candles courtesy of the local cat café. Rosie's owner Lila Brissett says: 'I have had lots of animals and they all live to a ripe age. It's about giving them lots of great love and care...'

2 JUNE

Thomas Hardy's cats

Thomas Hardy, born on this day in 1840, wrote some of Britain's best-loved novels, including *Tess of the d'Urbervilles* and *Far from the Madding Crowd* – and a very moving poem to his late cat, which brings a lump to readers' throats today. The author loved cats, owning around nine through his life. According to one biographer of Hardy, his Dorset home was a 'paradise of cats'. When a visitor enquired whether the cats all belonged to Hardy he replied: 'Oh dear, no, some of them are, and some are cats who come regularly to have tea, and some are still other cats, not invited by us, but who seem to find out about this time of day that tea will be going.'

The cats of Battersea

On this day in 1871, Battersea's first-ever committee meeting took place at the site where the London centre is based, 11 years after the charity was founded by Mary Tealby, a pioneer in animal welfare. In 1883, Battersea opened its doors to cats after a £500 donation from a Mr Richard Barlow Kennett, conditional on cats being welcome too. A total of 48 cats arrived at Battersea's doors in that year and, by the end of the century, an average of 500 cats a year were under its care. The original cattery, Whittington Lodge, is the world's first purpose-built cattery, and still stands at the London centre today. It is a heritage listed building. Nowadays Battersea helps care for thousands of cats across its centres each year.

4 JUNE

Dr Leon

When a stray kitten moved into the offices of the Order of Attorneys of Brazil to shelter from the rain and then decided to stay there, not everyone was thrilled. But as we all know, you can't outwit a good lawyer, so those members who liked having the cat around simply took him on the payroll and gave him a job. Dr Leon became the official 'Meet and Greet' welcoming committee to visitors stepping into the reception and even wore an official lanyard to prove it. After he passed away, his successor was announced on this day in 2020 in the form of Dr Leona. The lawyers at Dr Leon's former office have pledged they will continue to support animal rights thanks to these cats.

5 JUNE

Lucky

On this day in 2016 a cat called Lucky found herself in a very unlucky position – lost on the London Underground. Rescue cat Lucky accompanied her owner Lucy Duff everywhere and the pair were returning from a weekend away when, at Green Park station, someone bumped Lucky's cat carrier and it flew open. She fled, last seen running into the tunnel of the Victoria Line. Sympathetic TFL bosses agreed to launch a search for Lucky after the last train, allowing distraught Lucy to walk into the tunnels – to no avail. Then, a few days after Lucky went missing, an animal inspector rang. She had Lucky! 'Lucky was spotted by a TFL worker at 4 a.m., in the tunnel near Oxford Circus tube, pouncing on a mouse!' Lucy told a magazine. Lucky was covered in soot, dehydrated and hungry but, after sleeping solidly for three days, right as rain.

6 JUNE

Cattoos

Cats represent resilience – who else is said to have nine lives? – which is why many people choose to have a cat tattoo or even just an inking of a cat's paws. Since the days of Ancient Egypt, when cats were literally revered and killing one meant death for the offender, cats have held a special meaning for many. The Celtic peoples believed a black cat would ward off evil spirits while a raised cat paw symbolises good fortune in many cultures. Cristina Sabbia, singer with metal band Lacuna Coil, has her birthday today and is a lifelong lover of cats. She even has a black cat tattoo on her left forearm.

7 JUNE

Paisley, Isis, Feta & Scarlet P

Pop sensation Prince Rogers Nelson, whose career spanned four decades, loved cats, and these are just four of the felines he showered with love over the years. Paisley was a long-haired tortoiseshell named after the singer's home recording studio. He also appeared in the 1993 film *Grumpy Old Men* since some of the scenes were filmed at Paisley Park. Prince was born in Minneapolis to Mattie, a jazz singer and social worker, and John L. Nelson, a pianist and lyricist, on this day in 1958. One of the superstar's backup dancers was Cat Glover, who went on to release her own EP, *Catwoman*.

8 JUNE

Marmite

Jane Austen does not appear to have been much of a cat lover, with few mentions of cats appearing in her novels. 'Lord! Shall we sit and gape at each other as dull as cats?' asks a character in *Sense and Sensibility*. Not very flattering, but that hasn't stopped a black cat with a white bib making herself at home at Jane Austen's House in Hampshire, now a museum in the writer's honour. It is a truth universally acknowledged that cats are curious creatures and so Marmite, who lives nearby, has granted herself access all areas, sunbathing in the grounds on sunny June days and even snuggling on Jane's bed in winter. An uninvited guest Marmite may have been, but staff and visitors love her and she's now adopted the title of Official Museum Cat.

9 JUNE

Wendy

When pop star Britney Spears wanted to let her fans know that wedding bells were ringing, she posted an Instagram picture of her cat, Wendy, peering up at the camera from the folds of a crumpled wedding veil along with the caption 'Introducing Wendy ... and yes, this is the veil to my wedding dress.' On this day in 2022, Britney, then 40, married her fiancé of five years, Sam Asghari, in a lavish marquee filled with hundreds of chandeliers and erected in the grounds of their 20-acre, US$ 7.4 million Los Angeles home.

Tiber

Over a friendship nearly six decades long, and despite only meeting a handful of times, writers Sylvia Townsend Warner and David Garnett exchanged regular letters. In June 1973, they were both observing the behaviour of their cats and Garnett describes how his cat Tiber has a habit of coming up to him, playful and purring, while he reads or writes. They also share thoughts about the love they receive from their dear cats.

Cat Stamps

Cats have put their stamp on the world for centuries but, on this week in 2020, they put their stamp on envelopes too, as Royal Mail released a collection celebrating, in their words, 'the nation's most enigmatic pet'. Eight cats – a Siamese, Maine Coon, Bengal, British Shorthair, tabby, ginger, tabby and white and black and white – were featured in a variety of poses, including downward dog and, of course, napping. A very famous cat had featured in a previous Royal Mail stamp – the Cheshire Cat in the *Alice's Adventures in Wonderland* collection from 1979 – and Battersea itself was celebrated in a range of stamps featuring dogs and cats in 2010, the charity's 150th anniversary.

12 JUNE

Sox

A hitchhiking ginger cat from Herne Bay in Kent was described as having 'no boundaries' by the BBC – certainly Sox isn't contained by geographical boundaries. On this day in June 2023, Sox was resting up after the previous day's adventures. Deciding he fancied a day trip to the capital, Sox jumped into a stranger's car to Whitstable, where he sneaked into another car bound for London. Jacqui O'Connor was returning home after a day at the seaside when the stowaway appeared. 'We were driving down the motorway, singing along as you do and all of a sudden this head pops in between the two chairs,' she said. Sox's long-suffering owner Jessica Roe says she's had to pick Sox up from a variety of venues, including a kebab shop, an Amazon delivery truck and even a nightclub. She's now set up a Facebook page where people can report sightings of the travelling tabby and has bought him a tracking collar.

13 JUNE

Millie, Daisy & Pumpkin

Kat Dennings, animal activist and actor, has a cat called Millie, described as her doppelgänger. Kat's love affair with felines started in childhood when a stray cat, who she called Daisy, moved into the family home. By the time she was in her teens, a second stray, called Pumpkin, had also found her way to the household. So, it's not surprising that the way rescue Millie came into her life was pretty random too. 'I was in this pet place buying food for my dad's dog when I heard there were three rescue kittens who'd been found by an old lady when she opened up her garage door. I didn't even see Millie at first... She was the size of a teacup, fell asleep in my arms and so I bought everything she would need and took her home there and then.' No prizes for guessing who the *Thor* star will be celebrating her birthday with today.

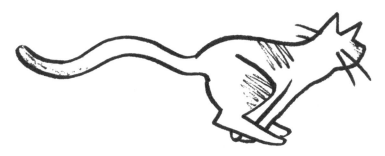

Daffy

Lucy Maud Montgomery, Canadian author of the *Anne of Green Gables* novels, the first of which was published this week in 1908, was a cat lover. In *Lucy Maud and the Cavendish Cat*, author Lynn Manuel draws from Montgomery's journals to write a story from the perspective of her cat Daffy, who was named after the daffodils in her garden, chosen from a farmer's litter and missed so much when Montgomery moved away to get married that Daffy travelled by rail to join her. 'Dogs are too good and unselfish. They make me feel uncomfortable. But cats are gloriously human,' Montgomery wrote in *Anne of the Island*, the third of the Anne books.

Henriëtte Ronner-Knip

Dutch artist Henriëtte Ronner-Knip, born in 1821 and apparently so talented she sold her first painting aged 15, was such a keen observer of cats she built her brood a glass-fronted studio to scamper around in as she was painting them. Certainly her works contain all the fun and personality that cats provide – a ginger and white kitten dances along a piano's keys, a great tabby lounges on an open book and a pair of kittens find, in a wicker basket, a set of keys to flick around. Sotheby's has auctioned several of Ronner-Knip's paintings of cats in the past few years including, in June 2020, one entitled *The Young Artist* and depicting a kitten climbing over an artist's palette.

Catmando

You've heard people say sometimes truth is stranger than fiction – and this is one of those cat stories that proves this to be the case. In 1999, the Monster Raving Loony Party, which was first established on this day in 1982, appointed a cat to serve as joint leader. He won the position fairly and squarely, garnering the exact same number of votes (125) as Alan 'Howling Laud' Hope who was voted, with Catmando, to take on the leadership role after the death of party founder Screaming Lord Sutch, that same year. Catmando served in office from 1999 until his own death in 2002.

Beryl Reid

British actor Beryl Reid, born on this day in 1919, wrote a book called *The Cat's Whiskers* about the adventures of the ten stray felines she shared her home with and sharing recipes that her brood loved. 'You never possess a cat; you are allowed to be in a cat's life which, of course, is a privilege,' she said. She also claimed that, during the Blitz, her cat could tell the difference between British and German planes flying overhead, hiding if they sensed an enemy aircraft. The BBC felt similarly. 'In the event of an air raid,' a public service information bulletin ran on the radio, 'Cats can take care of themselves . . . Your cat will probably meet you as you enter the air raid shelter.'

Machiavelli

The Disney Pixar animated film *Luca*, which was released in the UK on this day in 2021, tells the story of an underwater dweller who rises to the surface, befriends a fellow sea monster and takes on human form in order to spend a blissful summer in an Italian village. Unfortunately for Luca and co, Massimo, the one-armed fisherman, has a cat who is not taken in by their disguise as human boys. The cat, called Machiavelli, spends the whole film watching and even scuffling with the disguised sea creatures, knowing them to be a pair of fakes. Machiavelli, who bears a striking resemblance to Massimo, is eventually appeased by the sea creatures when they bribe him with fish.

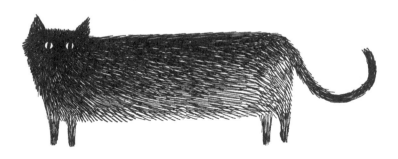

19 JUNE

Garfield

Garfield, ginger star of books, film and television, was born in a comic strip on this day in 1978 – apparently in the kitchen of an Italian restaurant where he developed a lifelong love of lasagne and pizza. Garfield is lazy and sarcastic, especially to his fur brother Odie the dog, and his main hobby is harassing the postman. A good example for other cats to follow? Certainly not, but many cat owners will sympathise with one of Garfield's traits that is universal – waking owner Jon up by standing on his head.

20 JUNE

Louis

Black and white rescue Louis moved in with resident cats Ginger and Snow after being adopted by Australia's first-ever winner of an Academy Award for Best Actress. American-born Australian Nicole Kidman, who celebrates her birthday today, won her Oscar in 2003 for her role as Bloomsbury Set author Virginia Woolf in the film *The Hours*. Virginia, as it happens, was a cat lover too and her extended essay *A Room of One's Own*, which was published in 1929 and which explored the impact of the First World War, social injustice and women's lack of free speech, featured a powerfully written scene where a tail-less Manx cat crosses the quadrangle at an Oxbridge University.

21 JUNE

Whitney

America's favourite pin-up girl, film star Betty Grable, starred in the musical romance *Coney Island*, which was cheering up American audiences when it opened this week in 1943. She famously had her legs insured by Lloyds of London for $250,000, but maybe her pristine white cat – Whitey or Whitney according to different reports – should have been insured too, or at the very least given a film role. Betty loved all animals – her cats were granted all access in her swish Hollywood home and she missed a meeting with Samuel Goldwyn, producer of *Guys and Dolls*, as her dog had broken its leg. Supposedly put out he'd been second preference to a pet, Goldwyn gave the role to someone else.

Bob

Bob was devoted to the writer and animal lover Charles Dickens and would sit with him as he wrote. He was the offspring of Williamina, the cat who belonged to Dickens's daughter Mamie, and was deaf. According to Mamie, he would follow her father about all day, just like a dog. One evening, as Charles was reading, the candle blew out. As he relit it, he absent-mindedly stroked Bob who, a few minutes, later, decided to put the candle out with his paw so he could get another fuss. 'Father was full of this anecdote when all met for breakfast the next morning,' wrote Mamie. Charles Dickens wrote *Oliver Twist*, which was made into a film directed by David Lean and first screened on this day in 1948.

23 JUNE

Margo Leadbetter

Scottish comedian and television presenter Susan Calman gives her rescue cats the most dignified names – take Margo Leadbetter who instructed Susan, on this day in 2023, to update her Twitter followers on her latest projects. 'I never argue with a cat,' Susan wrote. Susan introduced longhair tabby and white Margo Leadbetter to the world in January 2023 alongside another new arrival, DCI Vera Stanhope. 'We will carefully introduce them to our other girls when everyone is ready,' Susan wrote on Twitter. The other girls are Ruth Bader Ginsberg, Velma Dinkley, Daisy Faye Harper, Dr Abigail Bartlett and Olivia Pope. Margo is obviously settling right in. 'I've spent the past couple of days completing a massive spring clean,' Susan recently told her Instagram followers. 'Margo looked on with disdain as I found numerous cat toys discarded around the house. I collected them up and put them away in a box. An hour later they're all over the place again. Fair play. It's their house after all. I just live here and desperately seek their affection.'

24 JUNE

Pitch-invading black cat

It's rare for anyone to upstage Argentinian footballing legend Lionel Messi, born on this day in 1987, but a black cat did just that, crossing the footballer's path during a 2014 game between Messi's then club Barcelona and Elche. Play at Barcelona's Nou Camp was halted as the cat, pursued by stewards, raced around the pitch in front of 68,000 fans – but it did bring Messi luck because he went on to score two goals, and Barça beat Elche 3-0.

25 JUNE

Three Cool Cats

Cats have long been known for a certain style and panache, and it was this effortless cool that the Beatles attempted to channel during their 1962 audition with record company Decca. The band played their cover version 'Three Cool Cats', a song originally recorded by US group the Coasters. Sadly even this feline connection wasn't enough to secure the Fab Four a record deal, as Decca famously turned down the chance to sign them, and the rest is if course pop music history. The group's recording of the song did finally emerge on the band's *Anthology 1* collection in 1995. On this day in 1967, The Beatles performed 'All You Need Is Love' via live satellite link to 400 million viewers in 25 countries, as part of the history-making television production, *Our World*.

26 JUNE

Jimmy & Sassy

The Formula One racing driver Max Verstappen has two cats named Jimmy and Sassy but says, jokingly, he has thought about changing their names to Lewis and Toto – after fellow driver Lewis Hamilton, whose team principal is Toto Wolff. The Dutch and Belgian racing driver was the 2021 and 2022 Formula One World Champion and was the sport's youngest ever competitor when he started his career aged just 17, after starting karting in Belgium aged just 4. The reason we know he has cats is because he was taking part in a 24-hour simulated online race when he reported technical difficulties after Jimmy and Sassy decided to 'run through the sim' because the driver had forgotten to shut the door to his room.

27 JUNE

Mackerel

Japanese writer Haruki Murakami is one of the literary world's most celebrated novelists, publishing his books to international acclaim and popularity. And much to the approval of cat lovers the world over, our favourite animals play a central role in many of his books. In fact, in what is perhaps Murakami's most celebrated novel, *The Wind-up Bird Chronicle*, it's the search for a missing cat that underpins the entire story. When Toru Okada's cat (who has various names but is eventually called Mackerel) goes missing, it kicks off a twisting and turning sequence of events that includes a cast of fascinating characters and colourful literary metaphors. On this day in 1871 in Murakami's home country of Japan, the yen was introduced as the official currency.

28 JUNE

White Heather

In 1829, when she was ten and three quarters, a little girl wrote a story about Alice Lascelles' adventures at boarding school, chief of which was the mystery of who brought a cat – wearing a red ribbon bearing Alice's name – into the kitchen. The young author Alexandrina Victoria didn't know it at the time, but she would go on to become Queen Victoria, crowned on this day in 1838. Queen Victoria was an animal lover and many cats were resident at the palace, including the adored White Heather. Queen Victoria knitted her pet her a little blanket to play with and stipulated that, after her death, the cat's luxury life at Buckingham Palace should continue. Victoria also became Battersea's first Royal patron, in 1885.

29 JUNE

Elgar

Elgar is the feline companion to Ed Reardon, the 'author, pipe smoker, consummate fare-dodger and master of the abusive email' and eponymous star of radio sitcom *Ed Reardon's Week* on Radio 4, now in its 15th series. Ed, played by Christopher Douglas, is a grumpy, frustrated writer chasing literary acclaim and constantly bemoaning the modern world, with Elgar chipping in with a sympathetic meow. But the 15th series opened with some sad news – at the ripe old age of 25, Elgar had died. Reardon honoured him with a grave in the woods and a wind chime constructed with his old cat food tins.

30 JUNE

Manny

Born on this day in 1911, Ruskin Spear was an English artist and prolific painter of cats. He appreciated the feline form in all shapes, sizes and colours and his works include a tabby in *Sleeping Cat*, a large black and white in *Cat and Piano*, a marmalade in *Ginger Cat* and another black and white in *Cat in a Bovril Box*. Spear's' pet cats ranged from a Norwegian Forest to Manny, an old feral, but he said: 'Give me a moggy every time. Pedigrees are cats with birth certificates, aren't they?'

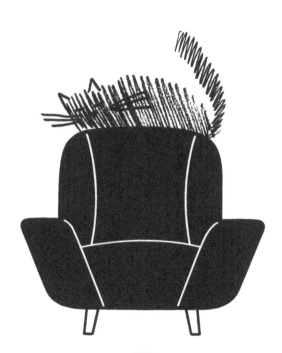

JULY

1 JULY

Browser

Browser is the Library Cat who gained fame for outlasting the Texas council member who tried to get rid of him. Browser had enjoyed his job as Library Cat since 2010 when he'd been adopted from a local shelter as a small kitten to work as pest control for a library in Texas. Browser soon became a much-loved fixture and member of the local community, and so when the town council decided to evict him – claiming the risk of allergies to library users as the grounds for his removal – there was such an outcry and such worldwide outrage, they had to take another vote to reverse the decision. The historic vote took place on this day in 2016. Browser was immediately reinstated, and the councillor who led the charge to remove him was voted out at the next election.

Blissa

Margot Robbie, the star of *Barbie* and *I, Tonya*, born on this day in 1990, owns a rescue dog called Boo Radley but, in a conversation with Karl Lagerfeld, had an interesting take on the differences between dog and cat lovers. 'It's about how you like to be loved,' she said. 'If you like dogs, you like big displays of outward devotion. Cats are like a sly, flirty grin across a bar.' Barbie herself is an animal lover and has shared her life with over 40 pets, including a white kitten called Blissa.

Hello Kitty

Hello Kitty is a fictional cat character who originated in Japan. She is a white cat with a red bow and no discernible mouth, and according to her back story, she lives in a London suburb with her twin sister, Mimmy, who helpfully wears a yellow bow so we can tell them apart. This little cat was first created in 1974 and the very first Hello Kitty product was a vinyl coin purse, which went on sale the following year. Originally targeted at pre-teen girls in Japan, Hello Kitty became such a huge worldwide phenomenon that customers soon included teens and adults. On this day in 2015, Sanrio announced a full-length theatrical feature film about Hello Kitty. There are also numerous Hello Kitty video games.

4 JULY

Peter

Louis Wain's whimsical sketches of cats showed them singing Christmas carols, on holiday and playing games, and were enormously popular among Victorian cat lovers. The popularity of Louis' work was thanks in part to the relatively new idea of cats as beloved pets, rather than something more wild – an attitude exemplified by the artist himself, who was himself the owner of a cat called Peter. Louis went on to forge a career painting scenes of wide-eyed cats in a variety of fun but surreal scenarios.

5 JULY

Foss

He may not have gone to sea in a beautiful pea-green boat with an owl, but English poet and illustrator Edward Lear's pussycat Foss certainly lived an interesting life, rolling on Lear's just-written manuscripts to dry the ink and stealing toast from visitors. He was so adored that, apparently, when Lear moved to Italy he instructed the architect of his new house to make it identical to his previous abode so Foss did not get confused. Lear, an exhibition of whose work at the Royal Academy of Arts was entering its final week on this day in 1985, used Foss as his model for the tabby in his illustrations for 'The Owl and the Pussy-cat'. When Foss died, he erected a headstone next to his grave, putting his age at 31 years – a bit of an exaggeration with the more likely, and very respectable, true number 16 or 17.

6 JULY

Black Cat

Mexican artist Frida Kahlo – born on this day in 1907 – frequently included cats in her work, in particular her much-admired self-portraits. But one particular cat held a deeper significance for the artist. Kahlo suffered health problems after being involved in a bus accident as a teenager, undergoing more than 30 operations and being bedridden for months on end – partly as a result of which she taught herself to paint. In 1949 she painted a self-portrait that featured a sleek black arching cat on her shoulder and a thorn necklace. The cat was a fictitious, symbolic creature rather than a particular pet. In 2021 the portrait sold for a record US$ 34.9 million, the highest sum paid at auction for a work by a Latin American artist. The painting was snapped up in under two minutes.

Ginger & Snow

Australian actor and mum of two cats Nicole Kidman says, 'I've always been a cat girl.' So it's no surprise that her two cats, Ginger and Snow, make lots of appearances on the Oscar-winning star's Instagram feed. The two cats are no strangers to the glamour of Hollywood themselves, since Nicole once took them along to the Telluride Film Festival for the premier of her 2018 crime film *Destroyer*. Nicole, who is married to singer Keith Urban, gave birth to the couple's first daughter on this day in 2008.

Tiger

The minister's cat, indeed — in the 1820s Pope Leo XII had a much-loved cat called Micetto, born as a stray in the Vatican and raised nestling in the folds of the Pope's robe. More recently Pope Benedict XVI, who resigned in 2013, was a cat lover, reportedly feeding the strays of Rome. And, this week in July 2020, a clerical cat called Tiger was cheering people up through the COVID-19 pandemic, sticking his paw in a jug during the Dean of Canterbury's online morning prayer service. Eight months later he was causing mayhem again, nibbling food during another broadcast.

Rollin' Stone

Singing superstar Bob Dylan is widely reported to be something of an animal lover, and he certainly references animals in many of his songs — including one called 'Cat's In The Well' on the album *Under the Sky*. But he went one step further on the album *Bringing It All Back Home*, released in 1965, appearing in the cover photo holding a small grey cat, reportedly known as Rollin' Stone, on his lap. On this day in 1962 Dylan recorded 'Blowin' In The Wind', one of his most famous songs and an enduring anthem for movements in support of peace and freedom.

10 JULY

Jack

Little Mix star Perrie Edwards, born on this day in 1993, is a real animal lover, sharing her life with dogs and cats. So, when she and footballer boyfriend Alex Oxlade-Chamberlain set up home together in 2019, he knew he had to score with her 14-year-old childhood black and white cat Jack. 'Time for these two to bond,' Perrie captioned a clip she shared on Instagram. Household harmony obviously blossomed, as Perrie and Alex had a baby in August 2021 before getting engaged the following June.

11 JULY

Felix

On this day in 2019, a cat called Felix published her second book – not bad for a kitten who started out hanging around Huddersfield train station in 2011, looking for a job. She spent her days at the station, catching mice and cheering weary passengers, and was soon promoted to Senior Pest Controller, her wages paid in cat treats. She now has a cat flap in the station barriers, an annual calendar, 22,000 followers on Twitter and an apprentice, Junior Pest Controller Bolt.

The Cat That Walked by Himself

In Rudyard Kipling's 'The Cat That Walked by Himself', first published this month in 1902 in *Ladies' Home Journal*, the animals of the Wet Wilds Woods are coaxed into the humans' cave with treats. The dog, in return for roast mutton, becomes the man's helpmate hunting; the horse, in exchange for hay, his steed; and the cow, again tempted to the humans' side by hay, the producer of milk. The cat is wary: 'He went back through the Wet Wild Woods, waving his wild tail and walking by his wild lone.' But he's not immune to the warm fire within the cave. So he shows the woman what he has to offer – catching mice and comforting her baby. A deal is struck. In return for catching mice and making the baby smile, he can come and go as he pleases.

India Bush

Miss India Bush belonged to American political royalty, being the cat of President George Bush and his wife, Laura. The ink black cat joined the family in 1991 when the couple's twin daughters, Barbara and Jenna, were just nine. At that time, George Bush Sr. owned the Texas Rangers baseball team and Barbara named the kitten after the nickname of star player Ruben Sierra. The cat moved with the family to the White House in 2001 and was a member of that family for almost two decades. India was born on this day in 1990 and when, as an adult, Barbara Bush gave *Vogue* magazine a tour of her home she showed off a collection of paintings of cats that had all been painted by her father, George.

14 JULY

Nero

Although perhaps more associated with dogs (their first album included a cover of a song called 'Walking the Dog'), veteran rockers the Rolling Stones clearly have a soft spot for cats too – as legendary frontman Mick Jagger proved. In 2021, Jagger shared an image on social media of himself posing with a tiny black kitten called Nero, the newest member of the Jagger family. It was on this day back in 1964 that his band scored their first ever UK number one hit, with their cover of the Bobby Womack song 'It's All Over Now'.

15 JULY

Bella, Yoda, Walter & Pebble

These four cats are never lonely because their owners, American actor Beth Stern and her husband Howard, are foster parents to cats in transit and on their way to new homes – which means the couple have as many as ten temporary rescue foster cats living with them at any one time. In fact, Beth, who is an animal activist and champion and who celebrates her birthday today, has fostered almost 1,000 cats over the years. The actor adds that surrounding herself with lots of furry felines has made her life so much better: 'It truly is the best thing in the world.'

Tommy

A friendly tabby cat called Tommy likes to make himself known to visitors to the sculpture park in the grounds of Thirsk Hall in North Yorkshire, especially if they are having a picnic and may have tasty titbits to share. Tommy is Cat of the Manor, living in Thirsk Hall with Daisy Bell, whose family have owned the Grade II house for 300 years, and her husband Bill, children Dexter and Oswald and Stella the dog. With 20 acres of grounds to roam every day, Tommy is living his best life and it's recently got even better with the opening of a glamping site in the grounds offering even more opportunities to socialise.

17 JULY

Hendrix

At the end of 2021, a loved-up Jennifer Lopez introduced her combined 320 million Twitter and Instagram followers to a new four-legged addition to her blended family, a cat called Hendrix. The little kitten was named after the American singer and songwriter Jimi Hendrix, who is regarded as one of the most influential guitar players the world has ever seen. Clearly a fan, Jennifer married her second-time-around love Ben Affleck in a romantic midnight wedding in Las Vegas on this day in 2022.

18 JULY

Louisa

Many a stray London cat must have gazed into the Kensington home of novelist William Makepeace Thackeray, born on this day in 1811, and envied his cat Louisa. She shared fish from his breakfast plate and spent her afternoons snuggled under his waistcoat, dozing. When he had to concentrate on writing and Louisa, in the manner of cats for time immemorial, caused a distraction, he picked her up gently and politely placed her outside his study door. The Thackeray family were also kind to stray cats, laying out a row of saucers for them to sup from.

19 JULY

Midnight

The 2004 film *Catwoman*, starring actor Halle Berry, was the latest outing for the character with cat-like powers. We wonder what Halle's own cat made of her owner's performance as the feline superhero. The film itself features an Egyptian Mau cat called Midnight, who appears to revive meek and mild artist Patience Phillips after she drowns – giving Patience all the cat-like attributes she needs to switch into her alter ego and go tackle the baddies.

20 JULY

Button and Eric

Television presenter Clare Balding is a committed advocate for animals, so it's appropriate that on this day in 2023 she was hosting a celebration for the 80th birthday of her friend and fellow animal lover, the *War Horse* author Michael Morpurgo. Clare and her wife radio presenter Alice Arnold had one feline family member – British Blue Button. Then, after Button had five kittens, they ended up with six! 'We stayed up all night to help deliver them. It was quite a responsibility having to oversee the births of these tiny things,' Clare said. The couple kept one of Button's kittens – the adorable Eric – while the others found happy homes with friends and family. Describing Eric, Clare wrote on Instagram: 'He's got that classic British Blue grumpy look when in fact he's not grumpy at all. He's very affectionate.'

Snowball

The writer Ernest Hemingway made no secret of his great love of cats and today the Hemingway House Museum in Key West, Florida, where the author lived in the 1930s, is home to over 40 cats – who are allowed to roam there freely but who are also offered protection under the terms of his will. Hemingway, whose first cat was called Snowball, admired cats for their independence and loved to give them interesting names like Princess Six-Toes and Feather Puss. What he liked best about cats, he wrote was their 'absolute raw emotional honesty'. Hemingway was born on this day in 1899.

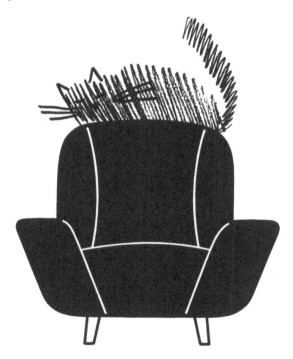

22 JULY

Kuching — City of Cats

Today is Sarawak Day, when the Malaysian state celebrates its independence. The capital of Sarawak is Kuching, also known as City of Cats because its name means literally that – cat. One story goes that, when the first Rajah of Sarawak first saw the city he asked its name. 'Kucing,' came the reply from a local who thought he was asking the word for a passing cat. Another theory is that the city is named after a local fruit called cat's eye. Whatever, Kuching has embraced its name with statues of cats of all shapes, sizes and colours popping up everywhere – the delightfully kitsch Great Cat of Kuching statue is especially popular with tourists. Kuching is also home to the Cat Museum, boasting over 4,000 feline-focused exhibits.

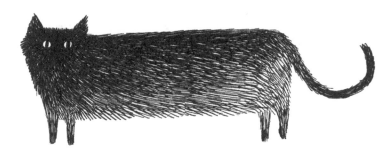

23 JULY

Crookshanks

Lion-like Crookshanks is Hermione Granger's pet cat in the *Harry Potter* books and films. The ginger cat, wanted by nobody due to his odd appearance, has an uncanny ability to solve problems without help. This could be thanks to something in his genes because Crookshanks is half Kneazle – a fictional breed that is claimed in the magical *Harry Potter* universe to possess higher than average intelligence and an ability to easily detect the presence of untrustworthy people. Actor Daniel Radcliffe, who plays *Harry Potter* in the film adaptations of the book, celebrates his birthday today.

24 JULY

Macak

On this day in 1939, a letter was winging its way across America from Serbian-American inventor Nikola Tesla, best known for inventing the modern alternating current electricity supply system, to his friend Pola Fotic, describing how his fascination with electricity was sparked, at the age of three, by his pet cat Macak. Stroking Macak's back one evening, Tesla witnessed: 'A miracle that made me speechless . . . my hand produced a shower of sparks loud enough to be heard all over the house.' His mother laughed: 'Stop playing with the cat. He might start a fire.'

25 JULY

Jacob

A miracle cat from Ayrshire called Jacob, who disappeared on this day in 2018, turned up eight days later after being trapped behind the grille of a car. Sharon Stirling had borrowed her dad's car and, when she returned it to him after eight days, he noticed a flash of white when he parked in the supermarket. Bending down to investigate, Jacob stared at him from behind the grille. Sharon, who'd been searching for Jacob high and low, panicked when she heard the news. Between her and her dad, the car had driven around 160km (100 miles) with Jacob in it! But mechanics from a local garage were able to free Jacob and a vet said that, although he'd lost a little weight and had a bruise on his nose, he was otherwise right as rain. In fact, it was probably a heavy rain shower that kept him hydrated and in such good health.

26 JULY

Stubbs

On this date in 1997, three-month-old orange tabby Stubbs marked his first week as honorary mayor of Talkeetna, Alaska. He would hold office for 20 years. Found in the carpark of Nagley's General Store (which was to become his mayoral office) and named for his missing tail, Stubbs showed little early political ambition but shot to power following a petition by local voters despairing at the calibre of human candidates. He became a tourist attraction, drawing countless letters during a two-decade tenure, along with dozens of daily visitors hoping for an audience. Each afternoon he would visit a nearby restaurant to sip catnip-laced water from a margarita glass.

27 JULY

Maximino

Opera-singing Max is a TikTok sensation after barging into owner Maura Navarrete's rendition of the classical song *El Majo Discreto* (The Discreet Beloved). Maura is a soprano and middle school choir teacher and was mid-rendition of the aria when Max pushed in front of her to steal the limelight and offer a musical, meowing performance of his own, at which point Maura collapses in giggles. The video went viral with over five million views and is well worth a watch. The song was composed by the Spanish composer Enrique Granados, who was born on this day in 1867.

28 JULY

Baldung's White Cat

The Renaissance marked a golden age of art, culture and music, a transitional period of European history typified by the work of painter Hans Baldung. Often associated with images of witchcraft, Baldung created a beautiful painting known as *Music*, in which a naked woman leans on a musical instrument, accompanied by a portly white cat to her side. Today is also marked by a different blend of music and art with a Renaissance theme, this time with a distinctly modern flavour – at midnight on this day in 2022, superstar Beyoncé released her album *Renaissance*.

29 JULY

Kevin

'Grayson's nice, but have you met my cat, Kevin?' So joked British psychotherapist and author Philippa Perry, wife of artist Grayson Perry, when asked the love of her life. Or was she joking? Black and white Kevin, who was adopted from Battersea in 2016, is the star of Philippa's Instagram page, stalking through the garden, napping, hiding in boxes, napping, sitting on top of a stile, napping, yawning and, on this day in 2022, climbing a tree. 'How to describe how you fall in love with a cat?' she wrote in a *Guardian* article in March 2018. 'First, the softness of their fur and their choice of your ankles to rub around makes you melt a bit. Secondly, you get used to their presence in your home and come to rely on it for company; and thirdly I think we project our love for ourselves on to our animals and believe it is coming back our way. I like to think Kevin really does love me. Whether he does or not, I love him.'

30 JULY

Tiger

Emily Brontë, born on this day in 1818, was a devoted animal lover – and cats were no exception. While she wrote *Wuthering Heights* her ginger and white cat Tiger was at her feet. He must have been a bold soul, because she painted a watercolour of him lying against her gigantic mastiff dog Keeper. In an essay called 'Le Chat' written in 1842, Emily wrote of her feelings for cats and dogs. 'We cannot stand up under comparison with the dog, he is infinitely too good,' she wrote. 'But the cat, although he differs in some physical traits, is extremely like us in disposition.'

Paddles

Ginger and white polydactyl cat Paddles was owned by Jacinda Ardern, the former New Zealand Prime Minister, and her partner, Clarke Gayford, so he soon became known as 'First Cat'. He had his own Twitter account and helped to raise awareness of the polydactyl condition, which is caused by a genetic mutation that means a cat has more toes than usual. Most cats have five toes on their front paws and four toes on their back paws, but polydactyl cats can have six (or more) toes on each paw. On this day in 1856, Christchurch in New Zealand was chartered as a city.

AUGUST

1 AUGUST

Mrs Chippy

Don't be fooled by the name – Mrs Chippy was actually a tough seafaring tomcat from the Glasgow docks who joined the crew of *Endurance*, led by explorer Ernest Shackleton, when they set sail from the East India Docks in London on this day in 1914, bound for the Antarctic. The cat was found curled up in one of the toolboxes by the ship's Master Carpenter, Henry (Harry) McNish – hence the name, chippy being slang for 'carpenter'. Shackleton was pleased to have a good mouser on board and the cat became known as the carpenter's 'Mrs' because the two were inseparable. Eventually, though, Mrs Chippy switched her allegiance to a 19-year-old stowaway called Perce Blackborow, who was discovered hiding on board and allowed to join the crew. He and Mrs Chippy became firm friends for the rest of the voyage.

2 AUGUST

Pixie

Family cat Pixie saved a child's life when she woke her owners in the middle of the night and ran frantically to their toddler's room, where they found their then 15-month-old daughter, April, choking on a piece of dried fruit she had eaten earlier that day. It was around 1 a.m. when April's parents Sophie and Mike were woken by the cat jumping on the bed, turning in circles and running to and from April's bedroom. Sophie followed the cat, saw her daughter was choking and called for Mike, who came and dislodged the fruit. Five-year-old Pixie, who lives with her family in Melksham, Wiltshire, was given an award for her lifesaving efforts and presented with her trophy at a ceremony in London on this day in 2017.

3 AUGUST

Sheldon

This morning, as every other in 2016, Sheldon the tuxedo cat from Southampton rose at dawn to prepare for the working day – having been taken in as a stray three years earlier by Anne Webster, he had just been promoted. Over the past months, Sheldon had made himself invaluable at the local B&M Store, welcoming customers and patrolling the aisles. So he was now given the title of Catsomer Services Manager with duties including testing out cat products and marketing and PR. In return, he had a box in the staff room for his belongings, a fancy swing chair installed at the store's entrance and adoration from customers, including one man who travelled all the way from America to meet him. 'The community cat, the people's puss and B&M's star employee – Sheldon loves everyone,' Lynne said. But, like any hard-working employee, Sheldon had to retire one day and, according to his Facebook page, is now feet up and slippers on, kicking back at a farm in Wales.

Jasper & Willow

A pair of rescue cats who spend their days comforting patients and visitors at a hospice in Haywards Heath, Sussex, were the first ever duo to jointly win the National Cat of the Year award. In 2022, siblings Jasper and Willow, who were adopted by the St Peter & St James Hospice four years earlier, won the Outstanding Rescue Cat category and then went on to scoop and share the prestigious title of Cat of the Year. Cat Jarvis, organiser of the annual award said: 'They are fantastic ambassadors for rescue cats showing just how friendly, caring and gentle they can be when given a second chance.'

Chicken

Chicken, the 10-year-old cat from Berkshire, was celebrating on this day in 2022 after winning a national award for helping his human, 11-year-old Elliot who is autistic, battle anxiety. 'They are normally together, whether it's cuddling under blankets or playing games, and their friendship is a huge source of comfort to Elliot,' Elliot's mum Jenny Abery said. 'They are just brilliant together and share a special bond which is priceless.' Elliot and Jenny attended an awards ceremony at the Savoy – Chicken stayed at home but was, reportedly, over the moon with the goodie bag and trophy she received.

6 AUGUST

Sam

Pop art pioneer Andy Warhol, born on this day in 1928, is known for printing repeated images of the same thing – soup cans and dollar signs, for example – and he adopted a similarly repetitive policy in the naming of his cats. Bar one, named Hester, they were all called Sam. In 1954, before he was famous, Warhol compiled a book of lithographs of his cats, so the various Sams have all achieved their 15 minutes of fame and more.

7 AUGUST

Slinky Malinky

The proud recipient of a National Cat of the Year Award on this day in 2014 was the brilliantly named Slinky Malinky Tomcat, who saved owner Janet Rawlinson's life when she slipped into a morphine-induced coma. Janet, who had been taking the pain medication for a chronic back problem, had been losing consciousness over five days but neighbours only realised they'd not seen her up and about for a while when Slinky started behaving oddly, scaling the walls and pawing at the windows. Janet was found unconscious and rushed to hospital and credits the cat with saving her life.

8 AUGUST

International Cat Day

Since 2002, 8 August has been celebrated as International Cat Day, which Battersea Dogs and Cats Home honoured in 2022 with tips on how to interact with felines by following the neat acronym C.A.T. – choice, attention and touch. The day is all about raising awareness of cat welfare and giving cats a lot of love, be that in the shape of toys or cuddles, when wanted. It's also a day when social media buzzes with pictures of cats – highlights in 2022 included Historic England introducing Budge 'Cat in Charge at Grade I-listed Norwich Cathedral'.

Pooni

All cat lovers know the stress of being away from their pets and the relief of being sent a photo by the cat-sitter, but imagine an age before the internet when such instant reassurance wasn't possible. In August 1961, Sir John Smyth and his wife Frances, on holiday in Majorca, had to wait for postcards to arrive from their beloved Siamese Pooni detailing her stay in the cattery. In his 1963 book *Beloved Cats* (illustrated by Frances), Sir John describes Pooni's missives. One reads: 'I am playing with my toys. Thank you very much for my nice letter which my Aunt Mary read to me. I have stopped chasing her feet.'

10 AUGUST

Mokuleiya (Moke), Sohalier & Thursday Adams

Having a cat is as relaxing as watching a fish aquarium according to cat lover Ian Somerhalder, who has three cats – Moke, Sohalia and Thursday Adams – with wife Nikki Reed. The *Lost* star spent more than five minutes sharing the joy of life with a cat on a YouTube video which has been viewed almost four million times. 'Cats have such imaginations,' he added. 'They will study a leaf or try and hide behind a sandal. They are very fun to watch and they also have that level of independence. They give you so much and their wellbeing is your wellbeing. It adds so much to your life. They really are beautiful, amazing fur balls!' The actor found Moke on the set of the hit TV show *Lost* and adopted him. The first episode of that ground-breaking drama aired today in 2005.

11 AUGUST

Shan

Gerald Ford, 38th president of the United States, took the Oath of Office this week in 1974, following the resignation of Richard Nixon, and moved into the White House with his wife Betty and family, including Shan – full name Shan Shein – a one-year-old Siamese cat belonging to Ford's daughter Susan. 'According to Susan Ford,' official records of the time revealed, 'Shan has slept with a heating pad since she was a baby. Shan will often sleep by Mrs Ford if she is taking an afternoon nap or relaxing, as Shan is very close to Mrs Ford as well as Susan.' Apparently Shan was quite discerning about which humans she would entertain but, Susan said, she made an exception for the President and often jumped into his lap.

12 AUGUST

Hurlyburlybuss

'A kitten was in the animal world what a rosebud is in the garden,' wrote the poet Robert Southey, born on this day in 1774, and he gave the cats who shared his life the most extravagant of names. Hurlyburlybuss also held the titles The Most Noble the Archduke Rumpelstiltzchen, Marquis Macbum, Earl Tomlemagne, Baron Raticide, Waowhler and Skaratch – thankfully he was known simply as Rumpel. Southey lived in the Lake District, at Greta Hall, and wrote a collection of stories about the feline occupants of the house, for his eldest daughter, Edith May. 'The Memoirs of the Cats of Greta Hall' is now held at Keswick Museum.

13 AUGUST

Good luck cats

When a Friday falls on the 13th of any month, it's considered unlucky – the sort of day on which your train will be cancelled or you'll spill coffee down your white shirt. There are a number of superstitions around cats too, but many of them concern good, not bad, luck. Spot a strange black cat on your porch in Scotland and look forward to a period of prosperity; in Holland, visitors are about to arrive if a cat washes behind its ears; and in Italy, hearing a cat sneezing is a good omen. If you're in Wales, feed a cat and you're guaranteed sunshine on your wedding day; and, in North Africa, hang an ear of corn behind the door and hope a cat nibbles it for luck. And enjoy sweet dreams of cats in the United States – apparently, dreaming of a white cat is a good omen.

14 AUGUST

Ziggy

On this day in 2022, a cat photo was posted online – one of the millions of photos of felines posted daily around the world. But this one, of a tabby and white spotted in a Hertfordshire park, brought about a reunion over a decade in the making. Cameron Mawditt was sitting on a bench with his friend when: 'We heard this little meow and out of the bushes comes this little cat,' he explains. 'It was really scared at first and wouldn't come near us.' But, as the cat grew bolder, they snapped some pictures for a local Facebook site, asking people if anyone recognised the cat. A local cat rescuer went to the park and scanned the cat and, a few hours later, a flabbergasted Ruth Orme received a call to say that her cat Ziggy, who had disappeared 11 years earlier, had now been found. 'He looks the same and acts the same,' she said when she was reunited with Ziggy. 'We can't tell if he recognises us because he was always such a friendly cat but he's been sitting on our laps and purring happily.'

15 AUGUST

Buttercup

It was mutual dislike between *The Hunger Games* heroine Katniss Everdeen (played in the film adaptation by Jennifer Lawrence) and Buttercup, the muddy yellow cat of her little sister, Primrose. Prim insisted her cat's coat was as bright and cheerful as the uplifting flowers he was named after, but Katniss was not convinced. Buttercup, who stayed with Prim throughout the books and the US$ 653.4 million film franchise, was played by a cat called Orion. Today is actor Jennifer's birthday.

Charles Bukowski

American rebel poet Charles Bukowski, dubbed 'a Laureate of American lowlife' by *Time* magazine, lived a pretty rock'n'roll life and his poetry readings sometimes descended into drunken brawls. But, in older age, he found contentment among cats. 'Having a bunch of cats around is good,' Bukowski, born on this day in 1920, wrote. 'If you're feeling bad, you just look at the cats, you'll feel better, because they know that everything is, just as it is. There's nothing to get excited about. They just know. They're saviours. The more cats you have, the longer you live. If you have a hundred cats, you'll live 10 times longer than if you have 10. Someday this will be discovered, and people will have a thousand cats and live forever.'

17 AUGUST

Black Cat Appreciation Day

Black cats have two days dedicated to them – today, 17 August, is Black Cat Appreciation Day and 27 October is National Black Cat Day. Black cats deserve to be honoured twice. Figures released in 2022 showed that black cats make up over 40 per cent of Battersea's feline admissions and they are often overlooked for adoption, possibly because of an old-fashioned association with bad luck – but people often overlook that black cats are associated with good luck too. In both Japan and the UK a black cat crossing your path supposedly brings good fortune, while on the Yorkshire coast fishermen's wives kept a black cat in the house in the belief that this would bring their husbands home safely.

18 AUGUST

Elvis

On this day in 1965, 'What's New Pussycat?' sung by Tom Jones, entered the UK charts where it would spend ten weeks, peaking at No. 11. Jones wasn't immediately taken with the tune, written by Burt Bacharach and Hal David, but over the years it's become a classic, covered by the Four Seasons and Alvin and the Chipmunks and appearing on the soundtrack of the 2001 film *Cats & Dogs*. And Jones must have crooned it many times to the Siamese cats he was often pictured with in the '60s, including one named after his friend Elvis.

19 AUGUST

Socks

There's a long history of dogs in the White House, but fewer cats have walked its corridors of power, so photographers were delighted when Socks Clinton, a personable cat happy to have his photo taken, appeared when Bill Clinton, born on this day in 1946, took office. It was quite a journey for Socks, who joined the Clintons as a stray, apparently jumping into Chelsea's arms, and he quickly became the celebrity cat of the '90s, even being recreated in Muppet form on television. And he was one of the first cats of the internet age. 'When I took office, only high energy physicists had ever heard of what is called the World Wide Web,' Bill Clinton said. 'Now even my cat has its own page.'

The Kitten

American comic poet Ogden Nash, born this week in 1902, was certainly poking fun at feline-kind with his poem 'The Kitten': 'The trouble with a kitten is THAT, eventually it becomes a CAT.' To celebrate the centenary of Ogden Nash's birth, the US postal service released, this week in 2002, a stamp in his honour featuring text from six of his poems, including 'The Kitten'.

Pooni

For a long period in the 1940s and '50s the Scottish island of Canna, one of the Small Isles in the Inner Hebrides and three hours from the mainland by ferry, had a feline ruler – Pooni, the Siamese. Cat lovers John Lorne Campbell and his wife Margaret Fay Shaw bought the island in 1938 and shared their home with cats of all breeds and colours. But Pooni was the king and Campbell, a historian of the Gaelic language, even wrote his biography, *The Book of Pooni*, binding it in leather. Included inside is a shopping list of items demanded by the cats, which they have all signed (possibly with a little help from John and Margaret). When Pooni died in 1956 John wrote in an emotional elegy: 'Now you have wow'd your last wow, roll'd your last roll, hook'd your last piece of cheese, and broken your last plate'. The National Trust for Scotland now cares for Canna but, in August 2018, launched an art trail to acknowledge its rightful rulers from yesteryear: 12 models of cats were dotted around the island to tell the Campbells' story. Of course, Pooni, with his distinct wonky ear, was at the centre of it, ruling the island once more.

22 AUGUST

Inside the Mind of a Cat

In this week in 2022, cat lovers were glued to a new Netflix documentary promising to teach them the psychology of their furry friends. In the hour-long doc, featuring plenty of slow-mo sequences capturing cats' grace of movement and exquisite sense of balance, cat scientists explored whether cats know their names (spoiler alert: yes), what their body language really means and why they get 'the zoomies' at night. 'They might be a lot smarter than we all think,' director Andy Mitchell admitted.

23 AUGUST

Mean-Eyed Cat

With his deep voice, edgy lyrics and preference for dark clothing, the Man in Black – legendary country singer Johnny Cash – may not seem a soft and cuddly cat lover, but appearances can be deceptive. He did, after all, sing about them in a number of songs – including on his moody 1958 tune, 'Mean-Eyed Cat'. Amidst Cash's talk of whistles blowin' and wheels a-turnin', the song tells the story of a woman who spends her partner's dwindling money reserves on cat food. While Johnny laments his partner's free-spending habits, most of us cat lovers will agree that cat food seems a perfectly reasonable thing to buy for any cat. On this day in 1969, Cash's famous live album, *Johnny Cash at San Quentin*, recorded at the prison of the same name, hit the number one spot in the US charts, where it would remain for four weeks.

24 AUGUST

Nacho & Stella Flay

Celebrity chef Bobby Flay has a cat called, appropriately enough, Nacho. An orange Maine Coon who has a sister called Stella, he has his own Instagram account with more than a quarter of a million followers (and rising). Together with his foodie owner, he is the founder of his own range of cat dinners. Nacho has his own indoor house called The Fish Market and spends a lot of time hanging out with his owner, including perching on his shoulder when he's cooking – licking his lips! The first episode of the American chef's TV show, *Beat Bobby Flay*, aired on this date in 2013.

25 AUGUST

Homer

In the spring of 1997, a Miami vet treated an abandoned male kitten who had lost both his eyes. She mentioned the three-week old kitten to a friend called Gwen Cooper, who offered the little cat a home on the spot. She named the kitten Homer, after the blind Greek poet credited as the author of the epic poems the *Iliad* and the *Odyssey*. Gwen already had two rescue cats, Scarlett and Vashti, and so little Homer soon settled in. One night, in 2000, Homer saved Gwen from harm and from losing her possessions when he attacked an armed home invader. Eventually Gwen and her cats moved to New York where on this day in 2009, Gwen published a book called *Homer's Odyssey: A Fearless Feline Tale, or How I Learned about Love and Life with a Blind Wonder Cat*, which was a heart-warming memoir about her life with Homer and her other cats. The book became an instant bestseller.

26 AUGUST

Towne

Melissa McCarthy, born on this day in 1970, co-starred with a black and white cat called Towne in the 2018 film *Can You Ever Forgive Me?* Towne – who plays a female cat called Jersey – is central to the plot as McCarthy's character forges letters by famous authors to pay the vet bills. The film's director described Towne as the Marlon Brando of cats and McCarthy, nominated for an Oscar for her role in the film, was also impressed by her co-star's acting abilities, saying: 'The first time I take him to the vet, while we are at the counter he sneezed. And I look at him and literally thought, "Are you kidding me? Are you pretending to be *sick*?" This cat is OUT-ACTING me!"

27 AUGUST

Crème Puff

Crème Puff was the oldest cat in history. The mixed tabby lived an amazing 38 years and 3 days and earned herself the Guinness World Record title for oldest known cat. Crème lived in Austin, Texas, with her owner, Jake Perry, and her cat brother, Granpa Rex Allen, who lived to 34 (*see* 1 February). The first *Guinness Book of Records* was published on this day in 1955.

28 AUGUST

Fred Wunpound

Plymouth-born black and white Fred Wunpound – so called because he was bought for £1 – was the last Royal Navy cat, working as rodent catcher and mascot on HMS *Hecate* from 1966 to 1974. Fred travelled 400,000km (250,000 miles) around the world, although on this date in 1970 he was back in his hometown preparing for a Navy Day to welcome visitors aboard the ship. Through his career, ended in 1974 by new laws to prevent rabies, Fred was promoted from Able Sea Cat to Leading Sea Cat Fred and achieved several accolades, including the Blue Nose Certificate for crossing the Arctic Circle – though the less said about an 'incident' in Brixham Fish Market, the better. He also received fan mail and even Valentine's cards from female cats impressed by his derring-do.

Sheila

Singer-songwriter and American stage and TV actor Lea Michele has a much-loved cat called Sheila, who will be celebrating her birthday with her today. Lea started her career as a child actor in musicals on Broadway, including the show *Les Misérables*. The 2012 film of this show starred a tuxedo cat who lives with the scoundrel innkeeper and his wife, played by British actress Helena Bonham Carter. Lea, who also starred as Rachel Berry in the TV hit *Glee*, is clearly obsessed with Sheila, and makes her the star of her Instagram pages. She told *Flare* magazine that Sheila is 'The greatest cat in the whole world!'

Madame Theophile

'Who can believe there is no soul behind those luminous eyes?' Who indeed? Certainly not the nineteenth-century French poet Théophile Gautier, born on this day in 1811. Gautier wrote a book called *Ménagerie Intime* about the pets who shared his life, including one great favourite Madame Theophile the cat. A reviewer wrote of her: 'She dwelt with him on terms of great intimacy, sleeping with him, sitting on the arm of his chair when he wrote, following him on his walks through the garden and always present at meals, when she sometimes stole attractive bits from his plate.'

31 AUGUST

Toby

On this day, Bank Holiday Monday in 2020, Toby the rescue cat was adopted by a loving family. So it was fitting that, exactly a year later, he was reunited with them after getting lost. Three months earlier, in June 2021, Karen Marshall was woken by her husband Ed, panicking. Toby, an indoor cat, had escaped through a window. For the next three months Karen and Ed searched everywhere for Toby, posting his photo all over social media. Then, on 31 August, Ed received a phone call from a vet – a stray had been handed in, its microchip checked, and it was Toby. There was only one strange thing – Toby was in Towcester, 180km (114 miles) from their home in Crewe. The most likely answer to the mystery of his epic journey is that he'd snuck on to a train in a railway depot near his home, and suddenly found himself on the move. 'Toby's more affectionate than before – his yearning to travel is spent, we think,' Karen said.

SEPTEMBER

1 SEPTEMBER

Sully

Australian cat owner Craig Geeves says his tabby, Sully, saved his life when she woke him at 1 a.m. on the morning of 1 September 2014 to alert him to the fire that destroyed his home. 'She was standing on my head screaming, the loudest scream I've ever heard from a cat. And then I smelt the smoke and jumped out of bed. She saved my life!' The firemen who put out the blaze agreed. And while they could not save Chris's home, Sully's alert meant they were able to prevent the fire from spreading to neighbouring properties.

2 SEPTEMBER

Taki

Detective novelist Raymond Chandler, author of *The Big Sleep*, which was made into a film starring Humphrey Bogart and Lauren Bacall, released in America this week in 1946, wrote a long letter to a friend about his black Persian cat Taki. His constant companion as he wrote, Taki adopted a role many people working from home today will recognise. 'She has been around me ever since I began to write,' Chandler relates, 'usually sitting on the paper I wanted to use or the copy I wanted to revise, sometimes leaning up against the typewriter and sometimes just quietly gazing out of the window from a corner of the desk, as much as to say, "The stuff you're doing's a waste of my time, bud."'

3 SEPTEMBER

Brillant

Louis XV, who became king of France this week in 1715, was a renowned cat lover and his pets enjoyed lives of luxury at the Palace of Versailles. Louis' esteem shows in the naming of one particular white Angora Brillant, meaning 'bright' or 'shiny'. Brillant was friendly and gentle and held a lofty position in affairs of state, reclining on a red velvet mat above the fireplace in the Council Room where the King discussed matters of state with his ministers. Louis XV also commissioned a painting of his imposing black cat Le Général, a departure from the paintings of dogs that had graced Versailles' walls during his father's reign.

4 SEPTEMBER

Room 8

When a playful, stray grey tabby wandered into Elysian Heights Elementary School, California, in 1952, delighted pupils named him after their classroom: Room 8. Little could they guess he would become a school fixture – and local celebrity – for 16 years, vanishing at term's end every summer but returning, without fail, each new academic year. Nobody knows where he spent the summer months – but so dependable was his autumn re-emergence, news cameras set up in school each September to capture it. During term times, Room 8 roamed corridors and classrooms, spreading joy and nuisance, sleeping on kids' desks and smudging chalkboards with his tail. Children took turns to pet and feed him. As his fame grew – via magazine features and even a TV documentary – he received thousands of fan letters from across the United States. He is immortalised in paintings, murals and a pawprint cast outside the school. Room 8's passing in 1968 prompted statewide obituaries. Did a school adopt a cat, pondered one, or did a cat adopt a school?

Nala, Zen & Mr Big

Brothers Nala and Zen were able to stay together when they were adopted by their famous owner, pop superstar and actor Cher, who has made no secret of her love of cats throughout her life. Her first cat was called Mr Big. She found him as a stray hiding under one of her tour trucks in Detroit. Cher was originally one half of the singing duo Sonny & Cher, who made their first-ever appearance in the UK on this day in 1965, singing at the 100 Club in London. They had made their name earlier in the year with the huge hit, 'I Got You Babe.'

Jones

He's been called one of the best film cats of all time and it's true that this ginger American shorthair cat – sometimes called Jonesy – had a thing or two to teach the humans in the *Alien* film franchise about survival: he was the only creature who faced the Alien multiple times and lived to tell the tale. Clearly a survivor, the cat (who was played by four different cat actors in the films) is also the protagonist of a book adaptation of *Alien*, called *Jonesy: Nine Lives on the Nostromo*. *Alien* was released in the UK on this day 1979.

7 SEPTEMBER

Nicodemus

Evan Rachel Wood, who celebrates her birthday today, has a black and white tuxedo cat called Nicodemus, a name which is comes from the Greek and means 'people's victory'. The *Westworld* star adopted her cat from a rescue shelter and swears that Nicodemus taught himself to use the toilet!

8 SEPTEMBER

Chairman & George

Animal lover and TV star Ellen DeGeneres and her actor wife Portia de Rossi adopt all their animals, including their two cats, Chairman and George. *The Ellen Show*, which ran for 19 years, first aired on this day in 2003, giving lots of feline-loving celebrities a chance to share their love for their cats as part of their interview. And Ellen herself often mentioned the joy her animals bring her, saying that they are 'the best companions that you can have'.

9 SEPTEMBER

Soumise

Born on this day in 1585, nobleman and clergyman Cardinal Richelieu was France's First Minister of State, living a life of great riches and splendour, which he shared with his 14 cats, who had their own quarters in his palace and special attendants to care for them. He was a ruthless leader, but his devotion to feline-kind displayed a softer side. Some of his favourites were jet-black Lucifer, Thisbe, Perruque and cuddle monster Soumise who was, apparently, his favourite. When Richelieu died, he left money for his cats in his will, naming a dedicated carer to cosset them so they could carry on living in the style to which they'd become accustomed.

Chief Mouser

It was Cardinal Thomas Wolsey, the former Lord High Chancellor of Great Britain, who first gave his cat this title in 1515 while he was in power and Henry VIII was on the throne. Wolsey, who was made Cardinal on this day in 1515, began a long line of cats serving in auspicious positions in government, with Chief Mouser to the Cabinet Office now the official title for the resident cat to the Prime Minister of the United Kingdom. The current Downing Street cat, who has served since 2011, is called Larry and was adopted from Battersea.

Flook

Queen Elizabeth II spent her life in the company of corgis, but that didn't stop her recognising the splendour of a cat on its 100th birthday – 100 in cat years that is; only 23 in human. In October 2006, Chris Evans from Cumbria wrote to the Queen to tell her his cat's centenary was approaching and a telegram duly arrived. 'I have watched Flook grow up from a kitten and I am very proud of her,' Mr Evans said. 'I really just sent the letter tongue in cheek and didn't expect anything back. But when I got the letter from Buckingham Palace I nearly fell over.' Flook was Mr Evans' longest reigning cat and, this week in 2015, Elizabeth became the UK's longest-serving British monarch, overtaking Queen Victoria.

Wingley

The New Zealand short story writer Katherine Mansfield, who moved to London at the age of 15, was a great cat lover and her letters are full of her cats' escapades. In a letter to a friend written on this day in 1921, she describes her joy that her little cat Wingley, who she mostly called Wing, had travelled, with another friend, to join her in Switzerland, where she was living because she was sick with tuberculosis and the weather was kinder than in England. Wingley arrived, she writes, with 'immense eyes after having flashed through all that landscape and it was several hours before the famous purr came into action . . . We expect him to write his reminisces shortly.'

13 SEPTEMBER

Mysouff 1

Animal-loving Alexandre Dumas, author of *The Three Musketeers*, shared his home with cats and was also a great friend to Parisian strays. Like many cat lovers before and since, he was convinced his cat Mysouff 1 – not to be confused with Mysouff 2 – knew when he was about to walk through the door and credited him with mystical powers. 'The cat, an aristocrat, merits our esteem, while the dog is only a scurvy type who got his position by low flatteries,' Dumas wrote. On this day in 1970, a station on the Paris Métro was renamed in Dumas' honour.

Little Danny

Appropriately enough for a former member of the Pussycat Dolls, radio presenter and *Strictly* runner-up Ashley Roberts, born on this day in 1981, is a cat lover. Ashley is one of Battersea's team of volunteer fosterers and once cared for a tabby kitten called Little Danny. 'He brightened up long days spent at home,' she said, 'and I loved watching him grow into a confident young cat before my eyes. I can't say a little piece of my heart didn't go with Danny when he went to live with his new family but knowing I had been his temporary mom and given him a home environment in which he could flourish was an amazing feeling.'

Tom

Sue had lived together with her cat Tom for 20 years, which means Sue had time to realise that Tom wasn't the most affectionate cat in the world. In fact, you might have found him somewhat aloof. And so, when Tom started pawing the back of her neck, Scunthorpe grandmother Sue thought something must be wrong with him and took him to the vet. She could never have imagined her 24-year-old cat was, as the vet suggested, trying to tell her that she was the one suffering a serious health problem. It turned out she had a cancerous tumour growing at the back of her neck. 'Tom saved my life,' she told reporters when her story made national news on this day.

16 SEPTEMBER

Cody

French composer Henri Sauguet wrote the scores for many films, including *Monelle*, the story of a friendship between a pianist and his protégé, released this week in France in 1948. Sauguet's cat Cody loved music too, specifically that of Debussy. When Cody heard Debussy being played on the piano, he'd roll around the floor in ecstasy, then leap on to the pianist's lap and adoringly lick the fingers that were producing the notes. When the pianist stopped playing, Cody would saunter off – but should the music strike up again, he returned and resumed his rolling and finger-licking show of appreciation. Debussy, himself a cat lover, would have been most flattered by these exuberant shows of support from his feline fan.

Champfleury

Born on this day in 1820, Champfleury was more than just a celebrated art critic in France, displaying his own creativity through writing novels. His most popular work *Les Chats*, published in 1869, was a collection of essays about cats and pictures of them, including one by Manet and another of Victor Hugo's cat Chanoine. Champfleury saw a strong bond between cats and artists, writing: 'Refined and delicate natures understand the cat. Women, poets and artists hold it in great esteem, for they recognise the exquisite delicacy of its nervous system; indeed, only coarse natures fail to discern the natural distinction of the cat.'

18 SEPTEMBER

Pete the Cat

Pete the Cat is simply too cool for school, or Christmas or anything else. In fact, if he got any more laid-back he'd probably be sleeping his way through the Twelve Days of Christmas, rather than 'grooving' his way through the festivities. Pete is a fictional cat and the star of a children's book called *Pete the Cat's 12 Groovy Days of Christmas* which is, of course, a play on the carol. The book, written by Kimberly and James Dean, was released on this day in 2018.

Jarvis P. Weasley

Pulp star Jarvis Cocker was born on this day in 1963 and has a rather handsome namesake in Houston, Texas – a cross-eyed ginger cat who, according to his social media biography 'rocks hard, lives fast, takes naps'. When Daria Kelly adopted a poorly kitten, found at a roadside, from a rescue shelter, she knew the cat needed an outlandish name to match his exuberant personality. Jarvis was chosen in honour of the Pulp frontman, Weasley after red-haired Ron in *Harry Potter* and the 'P' added for good measure. Now Jarvis is an internet celebrity but, Daria says, he takes the attention in his stride and it's all worth it for the pair to get across their message. 'Don't overlook rescue animals just because they're not as purrfect as pedigrees,' Daria says. 'Jarvis has enough personality for 100 posh pusses and more.'

Sophia Loren

Sophia Loren, one of the brightest stars of the Golden Age of Hollywood, popularised the cat eye make-up look in the 1950s – a flick of black eyeliner giving the eyes a feline quality. Born in Rome on this day in 1934, she was photographed with cats of all shapes and sizes over the years – Siamese, big grey fluffy Persians, tortoiseshells and gingers. Perhaps she was studying them for beauty tips. An archive of unseen photos of Hollywood stars with cats was recently unearthed in a filing cabinet showing Jane Fonda, Clint Eastwood, Audrey Hepburn and, of course, Sophia cuddling cats.

Sid and Nancy

Liam Gallagher, born on this day in 1972, took to Twitter to introduce his new tabby rescue kitten Sid in November 2018. A few months later, he adopted black and white Nancy. Liam's brother Noel also owns a cat, Boots. 'I do love the cat. Our cat is cool, it's like a dog, it'll come and sit on your lap and all that,' Noel said. And he reckons Boots is pretty smart.

22 SEPTEMBER

Jennie

Jennie the tabby is the eponymous hero of the 1950 children's novel by American author Paul Gallico. A lonely little boy called Peter is bewildered to find himself turned into a cat, but kind stray Jennie adopts him and tutors him in the ways of felines with advice, including 'When in doubt – wash!' Cat-lover Gallico apparently kept 23 cats at one time, so his descriptions of feline behaviour are drawn from observation – and love. 'Everything a cat is and does physically is to me beautiful, lovely, stimulating, attractive and an enchantment,' he wrote. Gallico was also the author of the novel *Mrs. 'Arris Goes to Paris*, which was made into a film premiered in London this week in 2022.

23 SEPTEMBER

Candide & Zadig

Elinor Glyn, whose romantic novels were considered rather scandalous in the first half of the twentieth century, adored her marmalade-coloured Russian cats Candide and Zadig, even taking them to literary luncheons with her. In 1927 Elinor's book *It* was made into a silent film starring Clara Bow – now credited with coining the term 'It girl'. Of her cats, Elinor's grandson and biographer Anthony Glyn wrote: 'They were beautiful, proud, independent creatures of enormous characters and "it", in many ways very like their mistress.' Elinor died on this day in 1943, and a photo of her playing with her cats hangs in the National Portrait Gallery.

24 SEPTEMBER

Mr Trunckles

During a TV interview, American actor and rescue advocate Jesse Eisenberg, said, 'I have two cats now but I'm on a list where they can deliver them to the house. To be a foster parent for cats is basically to have tenants coming in and out. I have a lot of cats, a lot of cat food, a lot of litter – and nothing else in the apartment.' Vegetarian Jesse is the star of *The Social Network* which tells the story of how Facebook came about, and which premiered on this day at the New York Film Festival in 2010. Mr Trunckles is the name of just one of his many rescue cats. (A group of cats, incidentally, is called a 'clowder'.)

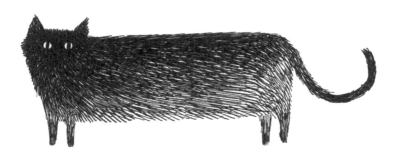

25 SEPTEMBER

Tom

The *Tom and Jerry* cartoon tells the story of the hapless cat Tom, who seems to be forever outwitted by his nemesis, the cunning little mouse Jerry. The duo launched in a Saturday morning slot on the American television network CBS on this day in 1965, before moving to Sunday two years later, where they remained until 17 September 1972. In the launch episode, Tom, who has been much loved by generations of children, was originally called Jasper. Historically, 'Tom and Jerry' was the phrase used to describe debauched young men given to drinking, gambling and riotous behaviour in nineteenth-century London.

26 SEPTEMBER

Fluffy

American sitcom *The Brady Bunch* has become a cultural icon, despite never being a critical success or ratings hit during its first run, from 1969 to 1974. But for cat lovers, it will forever remain a frustration as we mourn the fate of poor Fluffy, a handsome ginger cat introduced in an episode from the show's first series as the pet cat of the Brady girls – but never seen or mentioned again. Fluffy's run in the series, in which of course he proved himself the real star of the show, was short but sweet, and he doubtless lives on in the hearts of feline-loving fans of the series, which was first broadcast in the US on this day in 1969.

27 SEPTEMBER

Salem Saberhagen

This talking black cat is actually a 500-year-old witch, who was sentenced to spend 100 years as a cat by the Witches Council as a penalty for trying to take over the world. We first meet Salem in the pilot episode of the hit television show *Sabrina the Teenage Witch*, which first aired on this day in 1996. For the most part, Salem has a good heart and is a loyal friend to Sabrina, giving her guidance but also causing her some trouble in equal measure. We learn that Salem is originally from Mars. He is a very sensitive soul, cries frequently and dearly loves Sabrina, and calls her 'Sabreeny'. The show ran for 163 episodes across seven seasons.

28 SEPTEMBER

Charles

Charles: The Story of a Friendship is the touching tale of author and publisher Michael Joseph's 13-year-relationship with his cat, published in 1943. Even though the book is written in an unsentimental style, the warmth of their bond shines through. 'His friendship is not easily won but it is something worth having,' Joseph, born this week in 1897, writes. Their day began with Joseph sharing from his breakfast with Charles. 'For kindness and respect,' he wrote, 'he shared an abundant love.'

29 SEPTEMBER

Dirt

He was nobody's cat and everybody's friend and very aptly named because although his natural colouring was white and orange, Dirt was better known for his dirty-looking soot- and coal-stained coat after spending a lifetime sleeping on coal and rolling in soot. Born in a feral litter at the Nevada Northern Railways locomotive shop, Dirt was found left on his own hiding in a corner. The workers there enticed him out with strategically placed cans of tuna and from then on, he made the shop his home. The building of the Nevada Northern Railway was completed on this day — which was designated as Railroad Day — in 1906. The Nevada Northern railway is now a designated National Historic Landmark. Located in Ely, the workers there pride themselves today on recreating steam-era operations. They care for their mascot Dirt and in the winter make sure he has a heat pad to sleep on.

30 SEPTEMBER

Princess Annabelle, Munchkin & Cutesy

Paris Hilton, US TV personality and one of the world's first social media influencers, has three cats, Princess Annabelle, Munchkin and Cutesy. Paris adopted Princess Annabelle, who has piercing sky blue eyes, from a pet hospital in Santa Monica; Munchkin is also known as Shorty, while Cutesy, a Bengal, joined Paris and her husband, the American author and entrepreneur Carter Reum, in March 2023. Paris' TV show *My New BFF* debuted in the United States on this date in 2008.

OCTOBER

1 OCTOBER

Hamish McHamish

Hamish McHamish was the original 'cool cat about town'. Although he had an owner who cared for him and made sure he had regular veterinary checks, Hamish was a free-spirited ginger cat who liked to be out and about getting to know the residents of St Andrews, where he became something of a local celebrity. Eventually, he was to become the star of a book called *Hamish McHamish of St Andrews: Cool Cat About Town*. More recently, Hamish was the inspiration behind a series of *Hamish McHamish* children's books, which raise money for the Hamish Foundation.

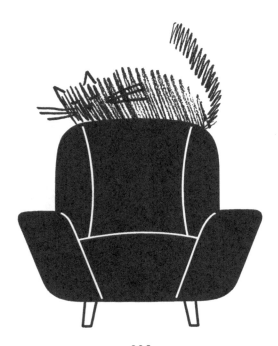

2 OCTOBER

Groucho

'A black cat crossing your path signifies that the animal is going somewhere.' So said a sceptical Groucho Marx, born on this day in 1890. The American comedian, famous for his owlish spectacles, bushy moustache and cigar, has appeared in several cat-related news stories over the years because he's had feline doppelgangers – minus the cigar, of course. One, Molly, in County Antrim, Northern Ireland, played on her unusual looks to stand out from the crowd in a rescue shelter while a vet's surgery in Alberta, Canada has their very own resident moustachioed Groucho. Groucho by name but not by nature: 'He is so unique that people stop by the clinic each week to have cuddles with him,' Sarah, office manager, says. 'He seems to know when people are sad and will get up from his bed and come over for a snuggle.'

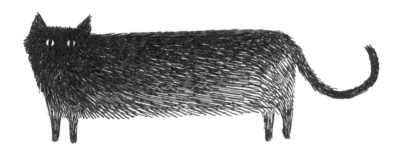

3 OCTOBER

Jambo

The British zoologist Desmond Morris was fascinated by cats from his childhood in Wiltshire, watching the farm cats stalking prey in the fields and suckling their kittens in the hayloft, and he was adopted by many strays through his life, including Jambo, found by him at the top of an apple tree. Morris, also famous for presenting *The Animals Roadshow*, wrote many books about felines, including *Catwatching and Cat Lore*, *Fantastic Cats* and *Cats in Art*, published this week in 2017 when Morris was in his mid-eighties. 'As a zoologist, I have had in my care, at one time or another, most members of the cat family, from great tigers to tiny tiger cats,' he wrote, expressing the hope for his reader that: 'You too will develop the urge to do some serious catwatching.'

4 OCTOBER

Tombili

Turkish cat Tombili had quite an impact on the residents and visitors of the city of Istanbul. Tombili liked to relax on the streets and was often seen adopting a human-like pose, leaning back on her elbows as she reclined on steps in the Ziverbey neighbourhood, looking like the coolest cat in the whole wide world. Before too long, a photo of her relaxing in this position went viral and soon after she died, a statue of Tombili was erected showing her in the same spot and that same distinctive pose. The now landmark artwork was inaugurated for World Wildlife Day on this day in 2016.

5 OCTOBER

Mitzy

Born this week in 1989, television presenter Stacey Solomon admitted on Twitter in 2018: 'I have become the cat lady I always feared . . . AND I LOVE IT!' Stacey understands the importance of putting your pet's needs first, though, explaining to fans in 2021 that her much-loved cat Mitzy had found himself a second home with a family down the road. 'At first I was really gutted and devastated,' she said. 'But there's enough Mitzy to go around. Now, he can brighten up two families instead of one.' Later Stacey moved to a new countryside home with husband Joe Swash and her brood, and even though it broke her heart, she said farewell to Mitzy, deciding it would be cruel to uproot him to the 'middle of nowhere'. She explained: 'We wish we could have brought Mitzy here but he became too settled with his new family down the road who also love him and wanted to take him on.' She wasn't without a feline presence in her life for long, however, as a stray black and white cat began visiting.

6 OCTOBER

Cardinal Wolsey's Cats

Historical figure Cardinal Wolsey is one of the main characters in Hilary Mantel's epic novel *Wolf Hall*, which won the Booker Prize on this date in 2009. Legend has it that, while he could be Machiavellian and ruthless in his dealings with people, he was a great champion of cats at a time when they were extremely unpopular. Apparently his cosseted cats accompanied him to meetings and church services and, while he was Chancellor to Henry VIII, his favourite black cat always sat beside him to discuss matters of state. There's an alternative view, though – that Wolsey's enemies portrayed him as a lover of cats to damage his reputation.

7 OCTOBER

Tom

The American wildlife photographer, bestselling author and television presenter Roger A. Caras published *A Cat is Watching: A Look at the Way Cats See Us* this week in 1989, and describes the extent of a cat's devotion and almost sixth sense when it comes to those they love. A cat called Tom took to hanging around Caras' house, fixated on his daughter Pamela, a college student. 'When Pamela was due home,' Caras writes, 'almost invariably Tom would be sitting on the front steps or at the end of the driveway waiting as she pulled in in her car. It happened far too often to be coincidence. Somehow that cat, whose actual identity and home we never learned, would know when Pamela was driving the two hundred or so miles from her college in New Jersey.'

8 OCTOBER

Jess

Black and white cat Jess is the beloved pet of children's television character Postman Pat. Always accompanying Pat on his rounds, Jess is an integral part of the story, appearing in all but one episode and even getting a mention in the programme's famous theme tune. On this day in 1965 London's Post Office Tower, at one time Britain's tallest building, was opened.

9 OCTOBER

Elvis, Mimi & Co

Pop legend and Beatles singer-songwriter John Lennon was mad about cats and had many during his lifetime, including Elvis, Tich, Sam, Tim, Mimi, Babaghi, Jesus, Major, Minor, Salt, Pepper, Gertrude, Alice, Misha, Sasha, Pyramus and Charo. No prizes for guessing who Elvis was named after, while Mimi was the namesake of the maternal aunt who raised John from the age of five. The singer also enjoyed sketching his cats with son Sean, and a few of those cat illustrations were used in his books. John was born this day in 1940.

10 OCTOBER

Anton and Cecil

Forget salty old sea-dogs – Anton and Cecil, fictional heroes of *Cats at Sea*, published this week in 2013, are two feline brothers who ride the ocean waves. Grey and wiry Anton likes to sleep, so being kidnapped into service as a mouser on a boat is rather a shock to the system; stocky, black Cecil, more adventurous, follows his brother out to sea. The *New York Times* praised the book for portraying the cats as 'authentically cat-like'. After conquering the sea, Anton and Cecil have more adventures in store through a further two books – on the railways in *Cats on Track* and in a hot air balloon in *Cats Aloft*.

11 OCTOBER

Camila Valenciana Azul, Cayetana, Antonio & Emilio

She might just have the fanciest of all fancy cat names, but then Camila Valenciana Azul lives with Hollywood royalty: Alec Baldwin and his wife Hilaria, whose family she joined in June 2022. Vegan Alec is unashamedly outspoken about animal rights and the importance of becoming vegan or vegetarian. Although he first launched his career with a role in the 1980 TV soap *The Doctors*, perhaps Alec's most iconic role was as Jack Donaghy in the TV series *30 Rock*, which first aired on this day in 2006.

12 OCTOBER

Faith & Panda

In 1936, a little tabby cat moved into St Augustine's and St Faith's Church in Watling Street in the City of London, close to St Paul's Cathedral. The verger wasn't at all happy about this, but the rector, Father Henry Ross, had a kindly heart and allowed the cat to stay, naming her Faith. A few years passed, the Second World War had started, and the rector noticed that Faith was spending a lot of time in the cellar. Upon investigation it was discovered that Faith was tending a single kitten, which they named Panda. A few nights later, there was an air raid, and the church and rectory were razed to the ground. The firemen asked Father Ross if anyone had been on the premises the previous night and he said just Faith and Panda. Sadly, he was told there was no way they would have survived amid the burning wreckage. Even so, he went searching for the mother cat and her kitten. He found them in the rubble, frightened but alive, and brought them both to safety. Faith had protected her kitten and on this day in 1945 she was awarded a medal for bravery.

Oliver & Company

The film *Oliver & Company* is a retelling of the Charles Dickens' story *Oliver Twist*, but with a cat called Oliver playing the lead role. The animated film, now a Disney classic, was released in the UK on this day in 1989. Oliver, who is voiced by Joey Lawrence, is a kitten who has been abandoned on the streets of New York. He is taken in by a group of dogs led by the Dodger (voiced by cat lover Billy Joel) who work for a ruffian called Fagin (voiced by Dom DeLuise). And so, feisty little orange tabby cat Oliver has to learn the way of the streets in order to survive.

Morrissey

Animal rights activist and comedian Russell Brand has eight cats, one of whom is called Jericho and another Morrissey, named after the British singer. When Russell was asked to bring some kind of tribute for Ellen DeGeneres to mark the tenth anniversary of hosting her talk show, he decided to make a cat video for her. Russell introduced Morrissey first via a portrait of the black and white cat which is hanging on the wall at his Oxfordshire home and then went to find the cat who was lounging on the sofa, ignoring the camera. Russell's book *Revolution* was published on this day in 2014.

15 OCTOBER

Holmes & Gracie

Songwriter Jason Mraz has always had cats. He grew up with a fluffy Ragdoll called Gracie and now has Holmes, who is an orange tabby. Jason says Holmes is his greatest critic because if a song that he is working on is bad, the cat makes his disdain known by simply leaving the room! Jason's debut studio album, *Waiting for my Rocket to Come*, was released on this day in 2002.

Cosmic Creepers

Cosmic Creepers is the black cat owned by Miss Eglantine Price, the apprentice witch and star of the 1971 Disney musical fantasy film *Bedknobs and Broomsticks*. We first meet Cosmic Creepers when Charlie, Carrie and Paul – the three children evacuated from London during the Second World War and taken in by Miss Price – arrive and assume the cat is stuffed. Until, that is, he startles them by hissing as they go by. In this original version, Eglantine Price is played by the late Angela Lansbury, who was born on this day in 1925. The film was based on two books written in the 1940s: *The Magic Bedknob; or, How to Become a Witch in Ten Easy Lessons* (1943) and *Bonfires and Broomsticks* (1947).

Mr Whiskers

Mr Whiskers belongs to Weird Girl and is an all-white fortune-telling cat who appears in Tim Burton's animated film *Frankenweenie* (2012). Weird Girl is one of Victor Frankenstein's classmates and she tells Victor that the cat has had a dream about him. Everyone knows that if Mr Whiskers dreams about you, something really BIG is going to happen to you – good or bad... Mr Whiskers looks as if he has stuck in paw in an electricity socket because all his fur stands on end and he has the spookiest white eyes that make him look even more ghoulish. The film was released in the UK on this day in 2012.

18 OCTOBER

Reggie

With Reggie taking the superhero lead and the others – Gonzo, Rizzo and Archie – standing in as understudies, these feline actors played Goose in the 2012 Marvel film *Eternals*, which also starred Gemma Chan, who played Sersi. In the original comic book, Goose is called Chewie, after Chewbacca from the *Star Wars* franchise. Chewie is the pet of Carol Danvers, who believes her pet is just a regular housecat – but, of course, she is mistaken, as he turns out to be a Flerken, a dangerous alien creature who can gobble up people! The film adaptation of the story was released on this day in 2012.

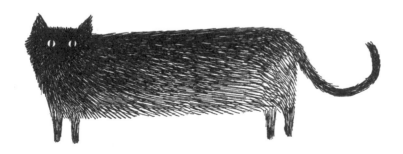

19 OCTOBER

Candy

One cat from the Isle of Man had a tale to tell this week in 2019, and her antics made headlines around the world. Voirrey Coole and her husband Nick were checking in at Isle of Man airport for a holiday to New York when a security guard quizzed her about the contents of her suitcase. 'There's nothing there but a travel blanket,' Voirrey said, confused, having kept it empty to bring back bargains. Growing increasingly concerned, she and Nick were ushered into a room where another security guard appeared to join the inquisition. Then Nick had a lightbulb moment. 'Is our cat Candy in there?' he asked. Candy had form on trying to sneak into suitcases. Sure enough, the security guard opened the case to reveal the black and white cat who scowled, annoyed her nap had been interrupted. The cat was out of the bag – and Voirrey's mum came to collect the stowaway.

20 OCTOBER

Tuxedo Stan

Although banned from running as a formal candidate because he did not have a birth certificate, Tuxedo Stan more than made up for his lack of credentials when he was put forward as a mayoral candidate in the 2012 municipal elections in the town of Halifax, Nova Scotia, Canada. He subsequently enjoyed a wave of celebrity endorsement, including animal lover and TV talk show host Ellen DeGeneres, who said she'd happily vote for the little black and white cat. Stan was put forward as head of the Tuxedo Party as a way of raising awareness of the local feral cat population, which was growing but which some felt was not being addressed by the local council. Stan's popularity forced the other candidates to consider the issue and all the profits raised from the cat's campaign were spent on the issue.

21 OCTOBER

Alex

You may have expected superstar musician Doja Cat to have a uniquely named cat, given her stage name. However, her cat has the ordinary (but still perfectly lovely) name Alex. Doja – who celebrates her birthday on 21 October – is really called Amala Ratna Zandile Dlamini, and Doja Cat is just her stage name. Alex is pure black with golden eyes and may possibly have provided some spark of inspiration behind the singer's 2014 EP hit, 'Purrr!' Doja says there's nothing mysterious about taking the name 'Cat' for her public persona. As she explains, 'I like cats!'

22 OCTOBER

Frisky

Frisky the tabby cat was a weekly visitor to the nation's sitting rooms throughout the 1990s – he appeared in the title sequence for *Coronation Street*. He was chosen for stardom from 5,000 feline hopefuls – whittled down to ten who appeared on ITV's *This Morning* and then, after viewers' votes, a final shortlist of five judged by *Corrie* stars like cat lover Hilda Ogden aka Jean Alexander. Frisky observed all the action on the street from his perch on the roof, including, on this day in 1993, Hazel telling Kevin that his wife Sally was having an affair. In all, Frisky appeared in the credits of over 1,000 episodes. His owner John Rimington from Leeds said: 'He was a fabulous, fun and outgoing cat – but many thought he was streetwise. He certainly wasn't. In real life he wasn't skulking round back yards – he had a converted castle to lounge around.'

23 OCTOBER

Nemo

On this day in 1964, Harold Wilson's family were settling into Downing Street after Labour narrowly won the General Election on 15 October. Wilson and his wife Mary had a Seal Point Siamese cat called Nemo, who by all accounts was doted on by his loving owners. He even accompanied the Wilsons on their holidays to their second home on the Isles of Scilly.

24 OCTOBER

Queen of the Mists

A retired and bespectacled schoolteacher in her sixties might not be the first person you would think of as having a daredevil streak – but in 1901, the first person ever to go over the Niagara Falls in a watertight wooden barrel was just that. And Annie Edson Taylor was even photographed after her historic adventure with a little cat sitting atop the specially made barrel. The cat's name has been lost in the mists of time, but the barrel was labelled 'Queen of the Mists'. Annie had apparently just lost her job as a teacher and so was looking for some way to make a living. It is a drop of 55m (180ft) from the top of the Falls to the bottom, not to mention the turbulent rapids, but Miss Taylor, who took the trip in her Sunday best dress, succeeded and spent the rest of her working life selling souvenirs of her great feat.

25 OCTOBER

Kitty Purry

Appropriately for a singer whose fans call themselves KatyCats, Katy Perry is a cat lover, even calling her perfume range, launched in 2010 in a cat-shaped bottle, Purr. Katy was born on this day in 1984, and her big feline love was Kitty Purry, who crawled through Katy's then-boyfriend's window, pregnant. 'This street cat became a mascot to many,' Katy wrote on Instagram when, heartbroken, she announced Kitty Purry's death in April 2020. Still, Katy's love for cats is in the genes. 'She is talking, but she thinks everything is a cat,' she said of her daughter Daisy Dove in 2021. 'When a person will walk in she will say "Hi, gato!"'

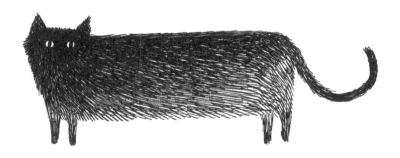

Pulcinella

Cats' meows may not be music to our ears when our furry friends scream at us for breakfast at dawn, but cats have played a melodious part in some fine classical music over the centuries. Legend has it that Italian composer Scarlatti, born on this day in 1685, credited his cat Pulcinella, who was fond of strutting along his harpsichord, with the composition of his Fugue in G Minor, popularly known as the *Cat's fugue*. Likewise Chopin's *Cat Waltz* was apparently inspired by a cat named Valdeck walking across the keys of his piano and inadvertently creating a melody that caught Chopin's ear.

Mog

Appearing in a series of children's books first published in the 1970s, Meg is a witch whose spells always seem to go wrong and Mog is her cat – only this is no classic witch's black cat, because Mog has great black and white stripes. The duo have a friend called Owl and the books, which were written by Helen Nicoll, chronicle their adventures. There are 24 books in the *Meg and Mog* series, which was turned into a TV show that first aired on this day in 2003. Actor Fay Ripley was the voice of Meg and actor Phil Cornwell voiced Mog.

28 OCTOBER

Goblin

Mary Russell, Duchess of Bedford, was a leading light of the cat world at the turn of the twentieth century (as were many aristocrats) and President of the National Cat Club, which, on this day in 1902 held a show at Crystal Palace with 550 entrants. The Duchess' favourite breed were Siamese, of which her cat Goblin was a fine example. Cat artist Louis Wain described meeting him on a visit to her house: 'On a fur rug a really royal Siamese cat sits, blinking in the glow and glint of the fire. His glossy coat is of a cream and mouse-brown colour, while his eyes are of a pale-blue mauve.' But the Duchess of Bedford was also a friend to strays, running, according to a newspaper article, a 'lodging house for poverty-stricken ones'.

29 OCTOBER

Society of Feline Artists

Old paintings of cats show how little their favourite pastimes and pursuits have changed over the centuries. In a painting by Belgian artist Charles van den Eycken, a kitten is climbing a wicker basket to peer inside; in another a group of kittens sleep all curled up together, ready for their next round of mischief. Plus ça change! In a painting by the printmaker and expressionist painter Franz Marc a cat relaxes, almost trance-like, in the arms of an adoring woman. London's Society of Feline Artists holds regular exhibitions to promote cats in art – on this day in 2021 their winter exhibition, online because of the pandemic, went on show featuring among others a relaxed black cat and, just like in ven den Eycken's day, two tabby kittens.

30 OCTOBER

Tommy

On this day in 1397, Richard (Dick) Whittington became Lord Mayor of London for the first time. This is still a popular pantomime story, but in fact it is the true story of a young man who went to London to seek his fortune, acquired a cat (often given the name Tommy, though this is unproven) who was such a good rat-catcher that Dick lent him to a ship's captain who, in turn, sold him on for a small fortune, sailed back to England and shared the spoils with Dick – who went on to become the Mayor of London not just once but three times. No wonder they say truth is often stranger than fiction.

31 OCTOBER

Charli, Frost, Mercy & Grey Kitty

Never mind keeping up with the Kardashian sisters, how about keeping up with all their pets? Kourtney has a cat called Charli and sister Khloe has one called Grey Kitty, whose arrival was celebrated with a cat-themed birthday party for Khloe's daughter, True. Grey Kitty is True's first pet (if you don't count her fish Nemo). And the mother-and-daughter pair also dressed up as cats for their 2022 Hallowe'en party on 31 October. Kim has an all-white male kitten called Frosty and Kylie has ginger cat Mercy.

NOVEMBER

1 NOVEMBER

The Amazing Maurice

The Amazing Maurice and His Educated Rodents is a children's fantasy novel written by Terry Pratchett. The book, which was first published on this day in 2001, features a cat called Maurice and a clan of rats who can talk. It is the 28th novel in the bestselling *Discworld* series and the very first to have been written for children. The book was turned into a film in 2022. The story is actually a new take on the old German legend of the Pied Piper of Hamlin and earned Pratchett the annual Carnegie Medal, awarded by British libraries to recognise the best children's books published in a given year. This was the author's first major award.

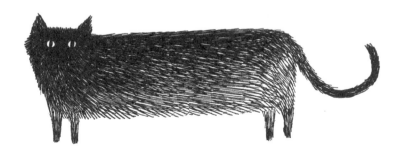

2 NOVEMBER

Misty

Praised for his sweet nature and creative name, Siamese cat Misty Malarky Ying Yang lived in the White House after Jimmy Carter won the presidential election on this day in 1976 as the favoured pet of his daughter Amy. Misty loved Amy and was often photographed with her but wasn't one for the big occasions, apparently fleeing when he wandered down the White House's grand staircase to be faced with a bank of photographers. He didn't complain about the tasty treats from the White House kitchen his role as First Cat brought him, however.

3 NOVEMBER

Kaspar

Rupert D'Oyly Carte, born on this day in 1876, took over as chairman of the Savoy Hotel in 1903, so must surely have dined several times with one of its most notable residents, Kaspar the sleek black cat. Kaspar is 60cm (2ft) tall, carved in wood in an elegant Art Deco style, and arrived at the Savoy in 1927 as the solution to an ongoing problem. Superstition dictated that tables of 13 were unlucky, but the practice of roping in waiting staff to make up numbers could lead to social awkwardness and a lack of people to serve food. Enter Kaspar – with a white napkin around his neck. What he lacks in conversation, he makes up for in confidentiality. To this day, never has a word of what he's heard under the Savoy's roof passed his lips.

4 NOVEMBER

Attlee

As the cat of House of Commons Speaker Sir Lindsay Hoyle, Attlee (named after the former PM), is the House of Commons meower. The tabby Maine Coon, introduced to the world in summer 2022, has a lot to live up to. Sir Lindsay, who was elected speaker on this day in 2019, previously had a cat called Patrick, who won Battersea's prestigious Purr Minister contest to find the top political cat in 2020. Patrick, also a Maine Coon, beat off tough opposition with his pledges of preventing fur flying in the chamber and impurrtiality. But newcomer Attlee seems up to the job, offering fans a behind-the-scenes glimpse into the House of Commons on his Instagram account, marching along Westminster's lush red carpets, gazing out at the River Thames and taking inspiration from his namesake's statue in Westminster's Members' Lobby. Order, order!

5 NOVEMBER

Purrfect

Purrfect, the Persian rescue cat who belongs to hit-maker CeeLo Green, landed her own lucrative endorsement deal after appearing with her doting owner on the US version of the popular TV talent show *The Voice*. After appearing on the show, Purrfect was signed up to do a remix of a jingle for a pet food company, which then relaunched its TV ad including the reworked jingle after a hiatus of 16 years. CeeLo released his third hit album, which included the hit 'Forget You', on this day in 2010. Delighted with the deal which the duo made in 2012, CeeLo said, 'That sultry purr of hers is perfect... Watch out cats!'

6 NOVEMBER

Tabby & Dixie

Known for his kind heart, President Abraham Lincoln, who was elected the 16th President of the United States on this day in 1860, had a great fondness for cats and it is said he often preferred their company to that of people. The two cats who moved into the White House with him were given to the new president by his secretary of state. He named them Tabby and Dixie and wouldn't think twice about feeding them from the table during formal political dinners. It's fair to say Lincoln doted on his cats, including several strays he took in. And he once told a friend, 'Dixie is smarter than my whole cabinet! And furthermore, she doesn't talk back!'

7 NOVEMBER

Lo-og

T. Rex frontman and pop legend Marc Bolan loved cats and named his after the influential record producer Andrew Loog Oldham. Glam rock superstar Bolan was posthumously inducted into the Rock & Roll Hall of Fame as a member of T. Rex by Beatle Ringo Starr on this day in 2020. There are lots of archive photos of a young Marc cuddling various kittens and cats, in which both the cats and the star look suitably stylish.

8 NOVEMBER

Nicholas

Here is another cat who was much beloved by a singing superstar. Nicholas belonged to 1960s' sensation Dusty Springfield, who made sure that her then 13-year-old feline companion would live out his days in luxury after she died in 1999. Legend tells that Dusty's will stated Nicholas should be fed a particular brand of food which had to be imported to Britain from the United States; that he should live in a 2.1m/7ft-tall indoor tree house lined with scratch pads; and that he should be serenaded to sleep each evening listening to her greatest pop hits. One of those hits, 'Son of a Preacher Man', was released on this day in 1968.

9 NOVEMBER

Kitty

On this day in 2012, Kitty the kitten and Buttons the Jack Russell puppy, who became best friends as tiny babies in Battersea Old Windsor and were so close they thought they were sisters, were off to their new home in Essex – together. The adorable pair stole the hearts of the nation when photos and videos of them playing, cuddling and sharing dinner emerged. Tiny tabby kitten Kitty was found at just one day old in a garden and taken to Battersea by a kind-hearted member of the public. To keep her company Battersea staff enlisted Buttons, a puppy who, as the runt of the litter, had been rejected by her mother and was being hand-reared by staff. An instant bond formed. 'Normally we'd hand-rear puppies and kittens separately, but we thought we could try putting them together, as they are both so young,' said a Battersea vet nurse. 'Luckily it's paid off, as they adore being with each other and do everything together – it's really very sweet.'

The Love Cats

On this day in 1983, the Cure performed their No. 10 single 'The Love Cats' on *Top of the Pops*, one of a few songs with a feline-themed title to grace the *TOTP* stage over the years. There was David Bowie's 'Cat People' in 1982; 'Stray Cat Strut', a hit for rockabilly rebels Stray Cats in 1981; and 'Cool for Cats' by Squeeze in 1979. Then there's Cat Stevens himself – now called Yusuf Islam – who performed in the *TOTP* studios 11 times. Rather disloyally for someone called Cat, his debut was with his 1966 single 'I Love My Dog'.

Koshka

When her soldier son asked for her help in getting an Afghan stray cat out of Afghanistan, American mum and quilter Helen Knott raised $3,000 by selling cat patterns to pay for the kitten's transportation costs. To this family Koshka meant everything because when Helen's son, Jesse, who was stationed in Afghanistan, tragically lost two of his best friends in the conflict, he struggled to find a reason to go on himself. At this point, Koshka, whom he had secretly rescued, would not leave him alone and Jesse, who now credits the cat with saving him, says he realised he couldn't give up. Koshka went to live with Helen in Oregon, where the following year, in 2010, he won a Cat of The Year award.

12 NOVEMBER

Mr Jinx

Mr Jinx might just have been the real star of the hit film *Meet the Parents*. Not only could he use the toilet and wave, but here was a cat who could do multiple tricks. Of course, in real life, he was played by not one but four different Himalayan cats, two of whom (Peanut and Charlie) now live permanently with the film's animal trainer. The comedy film, which starred Robert De Niro as the terrifying prospective father-in-law and Ben Stiller as the understandably terrified son-in-law-to-be, was released in the UK on this day in 2000.

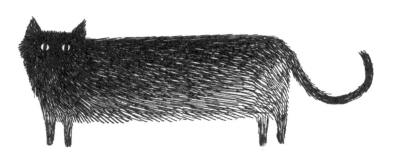

13 NOVEMBER

Vinny

Born on this day in 1955, American actress Whoopi Goldberg
is very much a cat lover so wasn't complaining after a famous
1984 Vanity Fair photo shoot in which she lay in a bath of milk:
'For three days, cats followed me.' In 2011 Whoopi, who played
the Cheshire Cat in a 1999 film of *Alice in Wonderland*, adopted a
Russian Blue kitten she named Vinny from a shelter. A passionate
animal advocate, Whoopi also shares her life with Bear, a blind
and deaf rescue dog.

Gravy

Would you like gravy with that? For some of the characters in the world's most famous paintings like the *Mona Lisa*, the answer is a resounding yes. Hannah Little from Nevada has been adding her rescue cat Gravy to some of the world's most famous paintings, putting him on the lap of the *Mona Lisa* and in Mary's arms in Giovanni Battista Salvi da Sassoferrato's *Madonna and Child*. Gravy also appears, staring beguilingly from a bridge, in one of the *Water Lilies* paintings by Monet, who was born on this day in 1840.

Missi

She's the cat whiskers, literally – Finnish Maine Coon Missi holds the Guinness World Record for the longest whiskers, measured at 19cm (7.48 inches) in 2005. Fellow feline record holders include Alexis from Austria, who can perform 26 tricks in one minute (very impressive because 99 per cent of cats refuse to perform even one) and Waffle the Warrior Cat, a tuxedo from California who, on 30 January 2018, performed the longest-ever jump by a cat of 2.1m (7ft). Guinness World Records Day, when people – and cats – the world over are encouraged to break as many records as possible, takes place every November. In 2012, it took place on this day – there were no challengers to Missi and her world-beating whiskers, though.

Luna & Oliver

In a 2022 survey carried out by the online platform *Daily Paws* for the top names for a cat, and published on this day, Luna was the top name for a female and Oliver the most popular name for a male. Luna saw off (in ascending order) Lily, Bella, Lucy, Nala, Callie, Kitty, Cleo, Willow and Chloe to take the No. 1 spot. Oliver, meanwhile, beat Milo, Leo, Charlie, Max, Loki, Simba, Jack, Ollie and Jasper to take the title. But lots of people apparently also like to name their cats after food, with Casserole, Frittata and Green Bean all getting a look in.

Mind's Cats

Known as the Raphael of Cats because of his extraordinary ability to capture the cat in his art, the Swiss painter Gottfried Mind (1768–1814) was a huge cat lover. Having spent time in an academy for poor children, Gottfried, who was so uneducated he could barely write his name, went to study with the great Sigmund Hendenberger, and on seeing a sketch the master had done of a cat proclaimed: 'That's no cat!' His mentor challenged him to do better and his love of painting cats was born. The painter, who died on this day in 1814 aged just 46, would often paint with a cat draped around his shoulders.

18 NOVEMBER

Domino & Bubbles

Emma Watson, who starred as Hermoine in the *Harry Potter* films, the fourth of which – *Harry Potter and the Goblet of Fire* – was released on this day in 2005, shares her life with two cats, Domino and Bubbles. Knowing the actress was a cat lover, BuzzFeed journalists decided to interview her alongside a gaggle of kittens on the press tour for the film *Beauty and the Beast* in 2017. 'I want them all,' she cried, struggling to concentrate on the interviewer's questions as the kittens gamboled all over her. 'I love that all of these guys are crazy and this one is just chill,' she said as a white kitten snuggled contentedly on her lap. 'I'm really going to struggle to say goodbye to this guy.'

19 NOVEMBER

Pyewacket

Running since 1939 the PATSY (Picture Animal Top Star of the Year) Awards are the Oscars for acting animals and, in 1959, Pyewacket the Siamese cat won, beating off stiff competition from Tonka the horse and Henry the rabbit. Pyewacket starred with Kim Novak and Jack Lemmon in *Bell, Book and Candle*, adapted from a play which opened on Broadway this week in 1950. Novak's character is a witch and Pyewacket her familiar, who casts a love spell on a handsome neighbour for her. Apparently Pyewacket had 12 doubles for the film. 'You can't teach one cat to do 12 tricks but you can teach 12 cats to do one trick each,' cat trainer Frank Inn, whose animals won over 40 PATSY Awards between them, explained.

20 NOVEMBER

Tao

Tao is the cat star of the 1963 film *The Incredible Journey*, which tells the story of three animals who decide to travel more than 250 miles to make their way back to their owners. Tao is the lone cat, travelling with his dog buddies Bodger, an ageing bull terrier, and Luath, a lively Labrador retriever. In the film, the animals are left by their owners to spend the summer with a family friend but, when he disappears on a camping trip of his own, the plucky trio decide to head for home, however difficult the journey may prove to be.

21 NOVEMBER

Nora

Born in 2004, Nora was a little grey tabby cat whose mother was a stray. Nora ended up in a shelter in New Jersey, USA, and the little kitten was adopted by a piano teacher called Betsy and her husband Bernard. The couple took the little kitty home and named her Nora after the British-born surrealist artist Leonora Carrington. Nora was soon meeting and greeting Betsy's music students. She liked to chase her own reflection on the shiny lids of the two grand pianos in the music room and especially liked the sound of the new Yamaha keyboard. After about a year, Nora astonished her owners by jumping up on the piano stool and doing what she had seen all the students doing. She used her paws to press the keys, and the sound that came out was actually quite pleasing. The first YouTube videos of Nora playing piano went viral and on this day in 2009 the little rescue, who had become quite the celebrity, won a Cat of the Year award.

Misha

Misha the rescue cat, who belongs to singer Billie Eilish, is named after the *Supernatural* actor Misha Collins. The actor only discovered he has a feline namesake when Billie's mom, Maggie, spilt the beans – after which he couldn't wait to go and tell his kids! 'Ocean Eyes' was released by Billie Eilish on SoundCloud in 2016 and became a viral hit, much to the surprise of Eilish and her collaborator and older brother Finneas. A music video followed, with a hugely popular video of Eilish performing a dance to the song coming next, released on 22 November of that year.

Mrs George Sanders' cat

James Mason, the English heartthrob of Hollywood's Golden Age, loved cats, even writing a book about them with his wife Pamela. Mason, who starred in Hitchcock's *North by Northwest*, released this week in 1959, shared his home with several cats – nine, at one count. 'If you're fond of cats,' Mason told a reporter, 'you're always getting more. Mrs George Sanders goes flitting off to Europe and asks if we'll take care of her cat. She comes back and sort of forgets her cat, so her cat becomes one of our cats.'

24 NOVEMBER

Shanti Om Bb

Shanti means 'peace' and so this little white cat, who belongs to animal lover singer Miley Cyrus (who also has dogs, horses and even pigs), brings spiritual vibes to the Cyrus household. On this day in 2013, the 'Wrecking Ball' singer performed her hit song at the American Music Awards with a giant, digitally animated ginger cat projected on the screen behind her, which lip-synched along to the song and garnered a huge amount of press attention.

Darwin's Cats

Naturalist and evolutionary biologist Charles Darwin, whose groundbreaking work on the theory of evolution *On the Origin of Species* was already selling out on this day in 1859, having only been published the day before, closely observed the behaviour of all animals, including cats. Comparing them with dogs he noted: 'Smiling and laughing are far less frequent in cats than in dogs ... their more subtle and subdued humour seldom necessitates laughter. It is generally more of a gentle teasing nature, not boisterous.'

Flock

Thanksgiving in 2020 was anything but dull for one family in Rochester, New York. Their cat, Flock, decided to climb a tree and got stuck there. Cat's claws are retractable but curve in such a way that while they have no problem climbing up a tree, they can only get down again if they reverse. This particular family called the fire services, only to be told they no longer respond to cat rescue calls, so the family spent 18 hours – the whole of their Thanksgiving celebration – trying to get Flock back down. They managed it, but only after the owner himself went up the tree and got stuck too. Which meant the fire brigade had to come to bring the pair back to safety.

Docket

On this day in 2013, a tribute from an artist to her beloved cat went on display to the public – a glass sculpture of Tracey Emin's grey and white cat Docket. When Docket had gone missing 11 years earlier, Tracey was distraught, but some of the posters she plastered round her neighbourhood were torn down by people after a quick buck and sold on. Fortunately Docket was found a week later in a derelict house. His other adventures included becoming stuck down a chest of drawers. But Docket took a dim view when Tracey had adventures of her own. 'When I'm ill or upset, he jumps up on to the bed to curl up close beside me,' she said. 'But if I'm in bed with a hangover he will have nothing to do with me.' Docket died, aged 19, in 2020 but lives on in his owner's work.

28 NOVEMBER

'Seacat' Simon

The Royal Navy regularly carried cats until they were banned in 1975 for health and safety reasons, and in 1948, Able Seacat Simon was the official captain's cat on HMS *Amethyst*. He won two awards for bravery, including the prestigious Dickin Medal, which almost always went to carrier pigeons or dogs, but which was awarded posthumously to Simon, who passed away on this day in 1949. Simon was hit by shrapnel when his ship was attacked and, although he survived that wound, he died the following year. He was buried with full military honours and a gravestone bearing his name.

29 NOVEMBER

Thomas

Cats love gardens, so it's appropriate that garden designer Gertrude Jekyll, born on this day in 1843, loved cats, living with four or five at any one time. Over the years, Jekyll's cats included Thomas, Mittens, Tavy, Toozle, Octavius, Pinkieboy and Tittlebait. Imagine the fun they must have had in the 11-acre garden at her Arts and Crafts home, Munstead Wood, in Surrey, recently saved for the nation by the National Trust. Her nephew Francis Jekyll wrote in his memoir of Gertrude that visitors to her home found her attention divided three ways: one part for the guest, 'one for the tea-things and one for Pinkieboy or Tittlebait.' An oil painting she created of her cat Thomas now hangs in Godalming Museum in Surrey, close to the house and garden she – and no doubt Thomas – loved.

30 NOVEMBER

Jock

Visitors to Chartwell, Winston Churchill's former home, are greeted by a ginger cat with white bib and socks – this is Jock, seventh in a line of Jocks to grace the stately home with their presence. Churchill, born on this day in 1874, loved cats and had many feline companions over the years but, on his 88th birthday, Jock the first, given by his chief private secretary Sir John 'Jock' Colville, entered his life. The ginger cat became a great favourite with Churchill – apparently dinner could not commence until he was seated at the table. So, after Churchill's death, when Chartwell passed to the National Trust, his family requested that a ginger Jock with white bib and socks should be in permanent residence. Jock VII, the current incumbent, was a six-month old rescue kitten when he moved to Chartwell upon the retirement of Jock VI but was soon lording it around, overseeing the work of the gardeners and reclining on the sofa after a day inspecting the grounds.

DECEMBER

1 DECEMBER

Catwoman

Born on this day in 1988, Zoë Kravitz played Catwoman in the 2022 film *The Batman* and really communed with cats to properly inhabit the role. 'They tried to get me to know the cats that were Selina's cats, and it's funny, they would say "Training at 1:30, and then rehearsal at this time, and then cat time," and I was like, "What's cat time?" And it was putting me in a room with the cats that were going to be my cats,' Kravitz recounted. She turned heads at the film's New York premiere in March 2022, wearing a black dress by Oscar de la Renta with lace-up detailing and the silhouettes of two cats.

Top Cat

Bin-dwelling Top Cat, the indisputable leader of the gang, and his band of merry cats stamped their paws on our cultural landscape in the early 1960s and have been regular fixtures since with the cartoon series' catchy theme tune instantly recognisable. In an episode called 'Sergeant Top Cat', first broadcast in the United States this week in 1962, Top Cat makes such useful suggestions for policing on his alley he's made honorary sergeant. In the UK, the cartoon was renamed *Boss Cat* in the titles, so it did not cause confusion with a cat food brand. Top Cat wasn't renamed, though: 'Yes, he's the chief, he's a king, But above everything, He's the most tip top, Top Cat!'

Catatonic

Happy Birthday Tiffany Sarah Cornilia Haddish, who was born on this day in 1979. Actor and stand-up comedian Tiffany owns Catatonic, whose name she changed from Clementine. Catatonic was one of the kittens who starred in the 2016 comedy film *Keanu* (also known as *Cat Boys*) and who Tiffany then took home with her. The story follows the antics of the Allentown Brothers, who must infiltrate a gang to retrieve their stolen kitten, Keanu. The pet-loving actor, who also has two dogs, also voiced the role of a dog, spirited Shih Tzu Daisy, in *The Secret Life of Pets 2*.

4 DECEMBER

Colin's

Colin's cat made international headlines when she stowed away on a tanker and travelled almost 10,000km (6,200 miles) from her port home in New Zealand to South Korea. The tortoiseshell and white cat had been adopted by Colin when he was the manager of the Port Taranaki tanker terminal in New Plymouth, New Zealand. The tiny kitten, who'd been abandoned at the port ten years earlier, was so small she went everywhere with Colin. Her own name was Queenie, but everyone called her simply 'Colin's cat' and when he then retired back to Australia, she was known as simply 'Colin's'. A rescue mission was launched when port staff realised she had accidentally set sail and it was on this day in 2001 that it was announced the mission had been a success and Colin's would be flying home the following day.

5 DECEMBER

Jeoffrey

Jeoffrey was both a cat and muse belonging to the poet Christopher Smart, who wrote about him in his famous *Jubilate Agno* (1759–63) which was eventually set to music by the composer Benjamin Britten in his cantata *Rejoice in the Lamb*. Many famous classical music composers were cat lovers and there is even an opera called 'The English Cat', composed by Hans Werner Henze, in which almost every character is a cat. On this day in 1895, the New Haven Symphony Orchestra of Connecticut performed its first-ever classical concert.

6 DECEMBER

Figaro, Maddie, Theo & Addison

American actor and singer Mandy Moore has owned a number of rescue cats over the years, and pays close attention to their names. In a recent TV interview, Mandy admitted she and her musician husband, Taylor Goldsmith, had consulted a cat psychic over the name of one of their cats. The psychic suggested changing the cat's name from Fig to Figaro after which, says Mandy, the little black and white cat was a picture of happiness. The *This Is Us* 'mom' loves to sing to her cats and some of them – especially Figaro – even like to sing back. *This Is Us* premiered on this day in 2016.

Boo Boo

On this day in 1888, audiences were packing the Lyceum Theatre in London to watch Ellen Terry, Victorian England's most famous actress, play Lady Macbeth. A portrait of Ellen in full regalia in the role now hangs in Tate Britain. But, wicked as she may have been as Lady Macbeth, Terry was a pussycat when it came to her pets, including her tabby cat Boo Boo, who accompanied her between her London performances and Smallhythe Place, her country cottage in Kent, in a specially designed wicker basket. With two small windows, a domed lid, door and handle, the carrier, which is now on display at Smallhythe, might not be as aerodynamic as today's versions but it certainly looks secure.

Mary's Catte

Mary Queen of Scots, born on this day in 1542 and becoming Queen only six days later, was a famous dog lover, with one of her Skye terriers apparently hiding beneath her skirts when she was executed. But she must have had some regard for cats because she embroidered one in a tapestry she made while imprisoned. A Catte, as she labelled the creature, is a rather fearsome ginger tabby with thick whiskers like a tarantula's legs. Pity the poor mouse it is eyeing. Some believe that Mary saw herself as the mouse and red-headed Queen Elizabeth I, who would eventually order her execution, as the cat.

9 DECEMBER

Lucky, Peach & Fern

American actor Drew Barrymore makes no secret of her love of cats or her support for animal rescue and welfare charities. On one day Drew, who has 16.9 million Instagram followers, came home from the local rescue centre with her hands full and posted, 'If you can believe, my daughters and I went to rescue a cat and came home with three kittens in need'. The kittens were named Lucky, Peach and Fern.

10 DECEMBER

Suki

Cats are well-known as their owners' early morning wake-up calls, so it's appropriate that the woman who wakes the nation of a morning is a cat lover. Breakfast television host Susanna Reid, born on this day in 1970, has an adventurous black Battersea rescue cat called Suki. 'I marvel at my attachment to a creature that remains so independent and ignores me until she needs food or a warm spot for a nap,' Susanna wrote in a newspaper. Suki lost one of her nine lives after falling ill as a result of a probable scrap with a fox and another after going missing and becoming disoriented – but a vet scanned her microchip and reunited her with Susanna. 'But,' Susanna wrote, 'No matter how often Suki scares the living daylights out of me, I'll always adore her.'

11 DECEMBER

Harry Cat

Today we are remembering a brave New York cat, whose heroics made headlines on this day in 1899 and were recently rediscovered in old newspapers by American author and animal historian Peggy Gavan. Up until 10 December 1899 Harry had been an unremarkable cat, the laziest of three brothers and usually to be found snoozing on the rug in front of the dining room fireplace. Then Harry was hanging out in the smoking room with the house's boarders when one of them threw a lit match, aiming for a bowl but in fact inflaming the curtains. Harry leaped into action, springing from the rug, jumping on to the curtains and pulling them down so the boarders could throw them out of the window. His beautiful white fur was singed but, promoted to the favourite pet in the house, he quickly recovered. 'This cat makes a record as a brave firefighter,' proclaimed *New York World* on 11 December, alongside a pen and ink portrait of Harry.

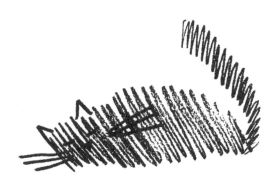

12 DECEMBER

Mr Snow

English physician and philosopher Erasmus Darwin, Charles Darwin's grandfather, and novelist and poet Anna Seward, born on this day in 1742, inhabited the form of their cats to exchange rather flirtatious letters. Darwin's Persian Snow lays out his advantages to Seward's Miss Po Felina. 'Derived from Persian kings,' he boasts, 'my snowy fur yet retains the whiteness and splendour of their ermine ... New milk, have I, in flowing abundance.' Miss Po Felina's reply is coquettish yet ultimately she declares: 'Marry you, Mr Snow, I'm afraid I cannot.' When the letters were published in Seward's posthumous biography of Darwin, eyebrows were raised over their intimate nature.

Sizi

'There are two means of refuge from the misery of life – music and cats.' So said the philosopher, doctor and humanitarian Albert Schweitzer, who won the Nobel Prize for Peace this week in 1952. Left-handed Schweitzer so adored his cat Sizi, rescued from a building site, that, should she choose to sleep on his left arm, he wrote prescriptions with his right. Sizi lived to be 23, so the old joke about doctor's having illegible handwriting was probably true for a long time in Schweitzer's case. 'Another cat, Piccolo, took her siestas on papers piled on Dr. Schweitzer's desk,' writes Ann Cottrell Free in her 1989 biography. 'Should they be in urgent need of his signature for immediate dispatch, well, too bad.'

Venus

On this date in 1962, the planet Venus, named after the Roman goddess of love and beauty, became the first of all the planets to be explored by spaceship after a craft called Mariner 2 flew by the planet to observe it. In one of Aesop's fables, a cat implores the goddess Venus to turn her into a woman so she can marry a man she's fallen in love with. Venus obliges – more than that, she makes the cat stunningly beautiful and the man is entranced. They marry, but the game is given away, rather, when a mouse slips into their boudoir and the woman, still a cat at heart, pounces.

15 DECEMBER

Orangey

One of the more heartbreaking scenes in the classic film *Breakfast at Tiffany's* is the scene in which a distraught Holly Golightly – played by ballerina-turned-film star Audrey Hepburn – turfs her cat out onto the New York side street in the rain, changes her mind and then gets drenched trying to find him again. The film was first released on this day in 1961. And the cat had no name because Holly felt she had no home. But in real life, the tabby who played him was called Orangey. 'If I could find a real-life place that made me feel like Tiffany's, then I'd buy some furniture and give the cat a home,' Holly says.

16 DECEMBER

Kitty-in-Boots

Bunnies might have been Beatrix Potter's muses of choice, but cats do crop up in her tales and, in 2015, a completely new story was discovered. *The Tale of Kitty-in-Boots* is a tale, Potter told her publisher in 1913, 'about a well-behaved prim black Kitty cat, who leads rather a double life'. But, due to the First World War, ill health and a family bereavement, she never finished it. Then, nearly six decades after her death, a draft of the tale was discovered among pieces in the V&A archives gifted by a collector. There was only one colour sketch of Kitty-in-Boots, but the artist Quentin Blake, born on this day in 1932 and famous for illustrating the Roald Dahl books, stepped in so the tale could be published over a century after Beatrix began it.

17 DECEMBER

Jacob

Bestselling children's author and Battersea ambassador Jacqueline Wilson, born on this day in 1945, wrote of the companionship her Battersea cat and dog gifted her during lockdown for an exclusive blog on Battersea's website. Her 12-year-old cat Jacob, she wrote, thrived. 'It's been a joyfully positive experience for Jacob,' she wrote. 'Up until recently he's always been very shy with strangers, hurrying to hide whenever the doorbell rang. He's gradually learnt to tolerate special friends, and even allows a little stroke now and then, but he's happier when it's just us. Therefore lockdown has been a joy for him, with no visitors at all. He can stride confidently round the whole house and when he pops out of his cat flap into the garden it's just as nature intended, a peaceful paradise. There's definitely a new spring to his step.'

18 DECEMBER

Sylvester

Sylvester the tuxedo cat is one of the main fictional characters in the kid's favourite animated series *Looney Tunes*. Produced by Warner Brothers, who wanted to emulate the success of Disney's Mickey Mouse cartoons, these were the shows that always ended with the memorable catchphrase 'That's all folks!'. Sylvester's full name is Sylvester J. Pussycat, Sr. He first appeared as a named *Looney Tune* character in the animated short 'Scaredy Cat', which was released on this day in 1948.

19 DECEMBER

Jason

Jason, a Blue Point Siamese, was the first *Blue Peter* cat in 1964, introduced by Valerie Singleton as a kitten sleeping in a basket with his brother and sister. 'He's very sweet,' she said. This week in 1975, Jason played the Cheshire Cat in the show's Christmas performance of *Alice in Blue Peter Land* with a voice strangely similar to John Noakes'. In 1976 silver-striped tabbies Jack and Jill made their debuts, appearing with their mother at just three weeks old, but they were shy and over the years became famous for scarpering whenever the camera was on them.

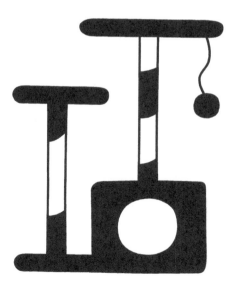

20 DECEMBER

Bastet

On this day in 1986, the Bangles' single 'Walk Like an Egyptian' hit No. 1 on the American charts. Cats certainly walk like Egyptians – they were revered in Ancient Egypt with their own goddess, Bastet. At her temple in Bubastis, a town on the Lower Nile, sacred cats were tended by priests in the courtyard and every year crowds made a pilgrimage by boat to the temple for her festival, a rowdy affair with much drunken cavorting on the streets.

Elvis

Emotional support cat Elvis has helped his feline foster mum, Beverly Pack, take care of over 100 kittens thanks to his loving nature. There's nothing Elvis likes more than a cuddle, so that's his job when the family have new arrivals who need reassurance. Elvis suffers from a mild form of cerebellar hypoplasia – sometimes called 'wobbly cat syndrome' – which affects his balance. Happily, the condition is not painful, but it does mean Elvis just needs a little extra support himself.

Lucifer

Lucifer is another famous cinema cat who happens to belong to Cinderella's wicked stepmother. We first meet this black and white kitty in the Disney animated classic of the fairy tale, which was released in the UK on this day in 1950. Lucifer, although a male tuxedo, was voiced by an uncredited June Foray and was said to have been based on animator Ward Kimball's own cat (although that cat was a calico). In the same way Cinderella's stepmother likes to taunt her stepdaughter, Lucifer likes to tease Cinderella's beloved and elderly dog Bruno, so you might say he really is a chip off the old block and just like his owner in more ways than one . . . the clue is probably in the name!

Big the Cat

Big the Cat is a large purple feline who appears in the *Sonic the Hedgehog* computer game franchise. Big really is a gentle giant – he's calm, chilled and easy-going and lives deep within Mystic Ruins. He might not be the smartest tool in the box, but he has a heart of pure gold and is one of Sonic's firmest allies. As well as being tough and super-strong, Big is also an expert fisherman. In fact, his favourite thing to do is to go fishing with his friend Froggy. Big doesn't go looking for action, but if one of his pals is in trouble he will be the first to leave the tranquillity of his normally peaceful life and leap to their defence. This cat first appeared in the *Sonic* franchise in the game *Sonic Adventure* – which was released on this day in 1998.

Chimney Cat

Someone was stuck up the chimney on Christmas Eve 2020 and it wasn't Santa. A family in Hampshire were confused to hear meowing from inside their chimney on 24 December, and called animal rescue. When an inspector removed the fireplace, a rather sooty black and white cat emerged. 'The cat was frightened and a little grumpy but thankfully wasn't injured,' rescuer Emily Stodart said. 'Although he did manage to leave sooty paw prints all over the family's light-coloured furniture.' Emily released the wannabe Santa Paws with a paper collar detailing the incident so his owners knew about his festive adventure.

25 DECEMBER

The First Cat Flap

Rumour has it that the inventor of the cat flap was none other than the genius Isaac Newton, who was born on Christmas Day in 1642 (O.S. dating system) and first formulated the theory of gravity. The story passed down is that Isaac would be busy working on his experiments at the University of Cambridge and got fed up with his cat and her kittens constantly scratching at the door asking to be let out or let in. So he called a local carpenter to cut two holes in the door — one for the mother cat and one for her babies — and, apparently, you can still see these two holes today.

26 DECEMBER

Choupette

A Boxing Day birthday for Jared Leto, the American actor acclaimed for his method acting, born on this date in 1971. And never did he more immerse himself in a character than in May 2023, when he dressed up as a fluffy white cat called Choupette for New York's Met Gala. As muse to the late fashion designer Karl Lagerfeld, Choupette, a white Birman, really was the cat that got the cream: she accompanyed him to events, sometimes by private jet, and, when at home in Paris, dined across from him every evening. 'Everything has to be fresh, otherwise Mademoiselle sits in front of her croquettes in sauce for three-quarters of an hour, giving me murderous looks,' Lagerfeld said. Since the fashion designer's death in 2019, Choupette has lived with Lagerfeld's former housekeeper in Paris, but she kept a watchful cat's eye on fashions at the Met Gala and, on her Instagram account, she awarded Jared Leto 100/10 for his Met Gala outfit, asking: 'Do I have a twin somewhere?'

27 DECEMBER

DC

A cat quite rightly takes centre stage in the 1965 comedy thriller *That Darn Cat!*, which explores the exploits and adventures of a streetwise tomcat known as Darn Cat, or DC for short. Darn Cat belongs to sisters Ingrid and Patricia, and spends his evenings walking the streets of his town, teasing the local dogs and marking cars with his muddy pawprints. But Darn Cat soon becomes the central character in an unlikely plot involving bank robbers, kidnapping and an FBI surveillance mission. The film was shown at Radio City Music Hall as part of its 1965 Great Christmas Show. The well-known New York City venue opened its doors to the public for the first time on this day in 1932.

28 DECEMBER

The Aristocats

It has more than stood the test of time as one of the all-time greatest family Christmas films of the last 50 years, and each year a new generation will settle on the sofa to watch the adventures of a family of Parisian cats trying to get home after being kidnapped by a jealous butler who wants to get his hands on the family fortune they are set to inherit. This Disney classic was first released in the UK on this day in 1970. Made for what is now the tiny budget of US$ 4 million, the film grossed US$ 191 million at the box office worldwide. Clearly a hit with cat lovers the world over.

29 DECEMBER

Arturo, Max & Otis

Actors Alison Brie and her husband, Dave Franco, are both devoted cat lovers and currently have Arturo, Max and Otis. Today is Alison's birthday. Film-maker Dave is the youngest of the three Franco brothers (James and Tom are both older than Dave), all of whom are actors and all of whom love cats. James has a cat called Zelda, and Tom even starred in a TV series called *Action Nat and the Cat*.

30 DECEMBER

Hinse

Sir Walter Scott was a dog lover but his tabby tom cat, the wonderfully named Hinse of Hinsefeldt, ruled the roost, taking a swipe at any dog he felt deserved it. A famous painting of the author of *Rob Roy*, published on this day in 1817, shows Hinse sprawled beside Scott at his desk and looking down at the dog at his feet. Hinse's other favourite spot, apparently, was at the top of the ladder in Scott's library. 'Cats are a mysterious kind of folk,' Scott said. 'There's more passing in their minds than we can be aware of.'

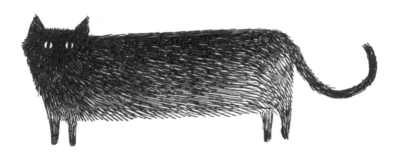

31 DECEMBER

Velma

The American actor and singer Debby Ryan, who is best known for starring as Bailey Pickett in the Disney Channel series *The Suite Life on Deck*, is the owner of pet cat Velma. The Disney star, who started acting at the age of seven, first shot to fame in *Barney & Friends*, which first aired in 1995. Debbie married her husband, actor Josh Dun, on New Year's Eve in 2019.

First published in 2023 by Welbeck.
This edition published in 2024 by Welbeck.
An Imprint of HEADLINE PUBLISHING GROUP

Design and layout © 2023 Carlton Books Limited
Text © 2023 Carlton Books Limited

Produced under license from Battersea Dogs Home Limited to go towards supporting
the work of Battersea Dogs & Cats Home (registered charity no 206394). For all
licensed products sold by Welbeck across their Battersea range, Welbeck will donate
a minimum of £20,000 plus VAT in royalties to Battersea Dogs Home Limited, which
gives its profits to Battersea Dogs & Cats Home.
battersea.org.uk

Text by Susan Clark and Jane Common, except 4 April, 27 Mar, 24 May, 25, 27 June, 14
July, 23 Aug, 26 Sept, 8 Oct, 27 Dec by Carlton Books Limited

Cataloguing in Publication Data is available from the British Library

ISBN 9781035425549

Printed and bound in the UK

FSC
MIX
Paper | Supporting
responsible forestry
FSC® C104740

HEADLINE PUBLISHING GROUP
An Hachette UK Company, Carmelite House
50 Victoria Embankment, London EC4Y 0DZ

The authorised representative in the EEA is Hachette Ireland, 8 Castlecourt
Centre, Dublin 15, D15 XTP3, Ireland (email: info@hbgi.ie)

www.headline.co.uk
www.hachette.co.uk